CREATIVE VIBES ONLY™

CreativeVibesOnly.Com

[MY] DAILY VIBE

A 365-DAY JOURNAL
FOR CREATIVES TO BE
THEIR HIGHEST AND BEST SELF

BY IAN DAVIS

(My) Daily Vibe
A 365-day journal for creatives to be their highest and best self.

A CREATIVE VIBES ONLY™ Journal

Copyright © 2020 by Ian Davis

All rights reserved. No part of this book may be reproduced or used in any manner without written permission of the copyright owner except for the use of quotations in a book review.

For more information, address: info@CreativeVibesOnly.com.

PO Box 1649
New York, NY 10027

First paperback edition December 2020

Cover designed by Booklerk
Edited By: Emily Smith and Ian Davis

ISBN 978-0-578-81801-6 (paperback)

Published by CREATIVE VIBES ONLY, LLC.
An imprint of Age of The Creative™

CreativeVibesOnly.com

To the writers, directors, musicians, painters, designers, filmmakers, illustrators, singers, producers, artists — ALL CREATIVES, this is created with love for you.

May this journal help your daily vibe, support your creativity and make you a better human.

May you be safe,
May you be happy in and with your creativity,
May you be healthy,
May your capabilities be free from pain,
suffering or sorrow.
May your gifts make room for you,
May you create
and use your creativity with ease.
May you be mindful, present, go within
and continue to help yourself.

– Ian D.

INCLUDED IN THE JOURNAL IS A FOUNDATION OF DAILY DEVELOPMENT WITH MINDFUL TOOLS, I BELIEVE ARE MOST ESSENTIAL FOR GROWTH, DEVELOPMENT AND OVERALL WELL-BEING AS A CREATIVE.

I HOPE YOU CAN USE THIS AS A GUIDEPOST TO TAP INTO YOUR POWER WITHIN TO GROW, BE MORE PRODUCTIVE, BE MORE INTENTIONAL IN YOUR CREATIVITY AND BE YOUR HIGHEST AND BEST SELF.

YOUR DEDICATION AND SINCERITY FOR GROWTH IS SEEN AND APPRECIATED.

I'M EXCITED TO JOURNEY WITH YOU IN THIS PROCESS.

WRITING THINGS DOWN IS EXTREMELY IMPORTANT IN THE CREATIVE PROCESS.

IT NOT ONLY CREATES ACCOUNTABILITY, BUT WRITING ALSO CREATES AND SENDS A VIBRATION TO THE UNIVERSE TO TRANSPIRE TO MAKE IT HAPPEN.

HOW YOU CAN USE THIS JOURNAL

TO DEVOTE TIME FOR YOURSELF AND

DEVELOP A DAILY PRACTICE FOR GROWTH:

1. DEDICATE A TIME OF THE DAY THAT WORKS BEST FOR YOUR SOLITUDE TO USE THIS JOURNAL.

2. FIND AN UNDISTURBED PLACE OR SPACE TO USE IT.

3. DETERMINE AND SET A FEASIBLE AMOUNT OF TIME TO DEDICATE TO THIS.

4. SET AND DETERMINE YOUR VIBE INTENTION FOR USING THIS JOURNAL.
   The next few pages will create the framework of the journal and help define your goals and your wellness

5. IMMERSE YOURSELF TO BE FULLY PRESENT THROUGH EACH SECTION,
   Feel and notice what arises without judgement

6. USE AND REPEAT DAILY.

[WATCH & LISTEN
TO A GUIDED
STEP-BY-STEP:]

CREATIVEVIBESONLY.COM/INTROJOURNAL

INTENTION(S)

"INTENTION IS THE CORE OF ALL CONSCIOUS LIFE. CONSCIOUS INTENTION COLORS AND MOVES EVERYTHING."

– HSING YUN

MERRIAM WEBSTER DEFINES INTENTION AS:
What one intends to do or bring about

WHAT DOES INTENTION MEAN TO YOU?
Spend a few minutes thinking about Intention(s) and what it means to you. As you think about it, write out and develop your own meaning and intention with this journal.

MERRIAM WEBSTER DEFINES WELLNESS AS:
The quality or state of being in good health especially as an actively sought goal.

WHAT DOES "WELLNESS" MEAN TO YOU?
Spend a few minutes thinking about wellness and what it means to you. As you think about it, write out and develop your own meaning.

GOALS

ARE EXTREMELY IMPORTANT IN THIS JOURNEY. IT'S THE BASELINE FOR YOUR GROWTH AND WHAT GROWTH COMES IN THIS PROCESS.

SET A GOAL.
CREATE.
REPEAT!

MERRIAM WEBSTER DEFINES A GOAL AS:
The terminal point of a race; the end toward which effort is directed.

SPEND A FEW MINUTES THINKING ABOUT HOW YOU DEFINE THE WORD "GOAL"
Additionally, think about and write your overall goal with your creativity and all the things you want to accomplish as an artist/creative. Where you want to go, who you want to work with, money you want to make, etc.

REVIEW YOUR LIST OF GOALS AND CATEGORIZE THIS LIST BASED ON PRIORITY OF: SHORT, MID, AND LONG-TERM.

SHORT:
(HAPPEN IMMEDIATELY – WITHIN 3 MONTHS)

....
....
....
....
....

MID:
(6-MONTHS - 2 YEARS)

....
....
....
....
....

LONG:
(2-5+ YEARS AND BEYOND)

....
....
....
....
....

MILESTONES

NOW SET SOME TIME-FRAMES/DATES THAT YOU CAN REALISTICALLY WORK BACK FROM TO KNOCK THESE GOALS OUT.

GOAL	TIME FRAME

IF THE TIME FRAME OR DATE IS 3 MONTHS AWAY, THINK ABOUT WHAT MILE-STONES YOU CAN PUT IN PLACE BETWEEN NOW AND THAT 3 MONTH DATE TO ACCOMPLISH THIS GOAL. WHAT FREQUENCY DOES THIS REQUIRE? A ONCE A DAY, ONCE A WEEK, ONCE EVERY TWO WEEKS OR ONCE A MONTH?

(NOT OVERWORKING OR SPREADING YOURSELF TOO THIN)

GOAL	TIME FRAME

"I AM" AFFIRMATIONS

ACCORDING TO MERRIAM WEBSTER

To "affirm" is to validate, confirm, assert as valid or state positively. When applied to your awareness, an affirmation is a statement of truth which one aspires to absorb into their life.

Affirmations are dynamic and practical — not wishful thinking. Affirmations can and do work because they are based on higher truths, we have yet to realize on a conscious level. According to Swami Kriyananda, "The greatest mistake people make is to belittle their own power to change themselves."

Self-improvement writer, Remez Sasson, says the repetition and corresponding mental images formed when saying affirmations help to change our subconscious mind.

The words "I am", which you consistently use to define who you are and what you are capable of, are the highest aspect of yourself.
Break lifelong habits of unwittingly besmirching this phrase.
Discontinue using pejorative labels to cast aspersions on yourself.
Always make your very first consideration the honoring of your Divinity.
This will allow you to rise to previously unimagined heights.

In affirming "I AM" you teach your outer self to accept the unlimited power of your inner spirit and the things you place in your imagination can become true for you.

Write down and affirm who you are. Speak and repeat your affirmations in a quiet space with concentration. The repetition of your affirmation allows change to your habit patterns and attitudes over which we normally have little control. Train your subconscious mind daily with use of your affirmations throughout the day and even in challenging times.

IF NOT NOW, WHEN?

- HILLEL THE ELDER

"10 STEPS TO PROTECT YOUR VIBE"

–VEX KING

1. AVOID GOSSIP AND DRAMA
2. LET GO OF ANYTHING YOU CAN'T CONTROL.
3. AVOID COMPARING YOURSELF TO OTHERS
4. KEEP YOUR FAITH LARGER THAN YOUR FEARS
5. DON'T DO ANYTHING THAT DOESN'T FEEL RIGHT
6. DON'T BE AFRAID TO SPEND SOME TIME ALONE
7. SPEAK KINDLY TO YOURSELF AND OTHER PEOPLE
8. PLEASE YOURSELF BEFORE TRYING TO PLEASE OTHERS
9. STAY AWAY FROM PEOPLE WHO DRAIN YOUR ENERGY
10. IGNORE ANY OPINIONS THAT DON'T ENHANCE YOUR LIFE

MY DAILY VIBE

"Perseverance is a great element of success. If you knock long enough and loud enough at the gate, you are to wake up somebody."

- HENRY WADSWORTH LONGFELLOW

Date: _____

(MY) WELL-BEING CHECK IN:
How I'm feeling

(MY) GRATITUDE TODAY:
What, who and things I'm grateful for

(MY) INTENTION FOR TODAY:
What I hope/intend to accomplish or even create today?

(MY) GOAL FOR WHAT I'M WORKING ON AND CREATING:

I AM:
My affirmation for today

ADDITIONAL NOTES, THOUGHTS, REFLECTIONS, VIBES AND GRATITUDE:

What are you doing to get closer to your goals, intentions, and wellness? What are the challenges you are facing? What else comes up during your day to reflect on?

MY DAILY VIBE

"A positive state of mind leads to more meaningful actions."

Date: _____

(MY) WELL-BEING CHECK IN:
How I'm feeling

....
....
....

(MY) GRATITUDE TODAY:
What, who and things I'm grateful for

....
....
....

(MY) INTENTION FOR TODAY:
What I hope/intend to accomplish or even create today?

....
....
....

(MY) GOAL FOR WHAT I'M WORKING ON AND CREATING:

....
....
....

I AM:
My affirmation for today

ADDITIONAL NOTES, THOUGHTS, REFLECTIONS, VIBES AND GRATITUDE:

What are you doing to get closer to your goals, intentions, and wellness? What are the challenges you are facing? What else comes up during your day to reflect on?

MY DAILY VIBE

"It's impossible," said pride. "It's risky," said experience. "it's pointless," said reason. "Give it a try," whispered the heart."

Date: _____

(MY) WELL-BEING CHECK IN:
How I'm feeling

....
....
....

(MY) GRATITUDE TODAY:
What, who and things I'm grateful for

....
....
....

(MY) INTENTION FOR TODAY:
What I hope/intend to accomplish or even create today?

....
....
....

(MY) GOAL FOR WHAT I'M WORKING ON AND CREATING:

....
....
....

I AM:
My affirmation for today

ADDITIONAL NOTES, THOUGHTS, REFLECTIONS, VIBES AND GRATITUDE:

What are you doing to get closer to your goals, intentions, and wellness? What are the challenges you are facing? What else comes up during your day to reflect on?

MY DAILY VIBE

"A flower does not think of competing with the flower next to it. It just blooms."

- ZEN SHIN

Date: _____

❤️ (MY) WELL-BEING CHECK IN:
How I'm feeling

....
....
....

🙌 (MY) GRATITUDE TODAY:
What, who and things I'm grateful for

....
....
....

📅 (MY) INTENTION FOR TODAY:
What I hope/intend to accomplish or even create today?

....
....
....

🎯 (MY) GOAL FOR WHAT I'M WORKING ON AND CREATING:

....
....
....

💪 I AM:
My affirmation for today

....

ADDITIONAL NOTES, THOUGHTS, REFLECTIONS, VIBES AND GRATITUDE:

What are you doing to get closer to your goals, intentions, and wellness? What are the challenges you are facing? What else comes up during your day to reflect on?

MY DAILY VIBE

"A goal is a dream with a deadline."
- NAPOLEAN HILL

Date: _____

(MY) WELL-BEING CHECK IN:
How I'm feeling

....
....
....

(MY) GRATITUDE TODAY:
What, who and things I'm grateful for

....
....
....

(MY) INTENTION FOR TODAY:
What I hope/intend to accomplish or even create today?

....
....
....

(MY) GOAL FOR WHAT I'M WORKING ON AND CREATING:

....
....
....

I AM:
My affirmation for today

....

ADDITIONAL NOTES, THOUGHTS, REFLECTIONS, VIBES AND GRATITUDE:

What are you doing to get closer to your goals, intentions, and wellness? What are the challenges you are facing? What else comes up during your day to reflect on?

MY DAILY VIBE

"A mind is like a parachute. It doesn't work if it is not open."
- FRANK ZAPPA

Date: _____

♡ (MY) WELL-BEING CHECK IN:
How I'm feeling

....
....
....

🙌 (MY) GRATITUDE TODAY:
What, who and things I'm grateful for

....
....
....

📅 (MY) INTENTION FOR TODAY:
What I hope/intend to accomplish or even create today?

....
....
....

🎯 (MY) GOAL FOR WHAT I'M WORKING ON AND CREATING:

....
....
....

💪 I AM:
My affirmation for today

....

ADDITIONAL NOTES, THOUGHTS, REFLECTIONS, VIBES AND GRATITUDE:

What are you doing to get closer to your goals, intentions, and wellness? What are the challenges you are facing? What else comes up during your day to reflect on?

MY DAILY VIBE

"Accept what God allows. There's always a reason."

Date: _____

❤️ (MY) WELL-BEING CHECK IN:
How I'm feeling

....
....
....

🙌 (MY) GRATITUDE TODAY:
What, who and things I'm grateful for

....
....
....

📅 (MY) INTENTION FOR TODAY:
What I hope/intend to accomplish or even create today?

....
....
....

🎯 (MY) GOAL FOR WHAT I'M WORKING ON AND CREATING:

....
....
....

💪 I AM:
My affirmation for today

....

ADDITIONAL NOTES, THOUGHTS, REFLECTIONS, VIBES AND GRATITUDE:

What are you doing to get closer to your goals, intentions, and wellness? What are the challenges you are facing? What else comes up during your day to reflect on?

MY DAILY VIBE

"All Happiness comes from awareness. The more we are conscious, the deeper the joy. Acceptance of pain, non-resistance, courage and endurance -- these open deep and perennial sources of real happiness, true bliss."

- NISARGADATTA MAHARAJ

Date: _____

(MY) WELL-BEING CHECK IN:
How I'm feeling

....
....
....

(MY) GRATITUDE TODAY:
What, who and things I'm grateful for

....
....
....

(MY) INTENTION FOR TODAY:
What I hope/intend to accomplish or even create today?

....
....
....

(MY) GOAL FOR WHAT I'M WORKING ON AND CREATING:

....
....
....

I AM:
My affirmation for today

ADDITIONAL NOTES, THOUGHTS, REFLECTIONS, VIBES AND GRATITUDE:

What are you doing to get closer to your goals, intentions, and wellness? What are the challenges you are facing? What else comes up during your day to reflect on?

MY DAILY VIBE

"All that we are is supremely divine. Trust the power of your energy, vibes and thoughts. Allow yourself to feel good about your greatness and your gifts. May you experience feelings of Good, abundance, joy, love, kindness and success."

— IAN DAVIS

Date: _____

(MY) WELL-BEING CHECK IN:
How I'm feeling

_____
_____
_____

(MY) GRATITUDE TODAY:
What, who and things I'm grateful for

_____
_____
_____

(MY) INTENTION FOR TODAY:
What I hope/intend to accomplish or even create today?

_____
_____
_____

(MY) GOAL FOR WHAT I'M WORKING ON AND CREATING:

_____
_____
_____

I AM:
My affirmation for today

_____

ADDITIONAL NOTES, THOUGHTS, REFLECTIONS, VIBES AND GRATITUDE:

What are you doing to get closer to your goals, intentions, and wellness? What are the challenges you are facing? What else comes up during your day to reflect on?

MY DAILY VIBE

"All the things that truly matter, beauty, love creativity, joy and inner peace arise beyond the mind."

— EKHART TOLLE

Date: _____

(MY) WELL-BEING CHECK IN:
How I'm feeling

(MY) GRATITUDE TODAY:
What, who and things I'm grateful for

(MY) INTENTION FOR TODAY:
What I hope/intend to accomplish or even create today?

(MY) GOAL FOR WHAT I'M WORKING ON AND CREATING:

I AM:
My affirmation for today

ADDITIONAL NOTES, THOUGHTS, REFLECTIONS, VIBES AND GRATITUDE:

What are you doing to get closer to your goals, intentions, and wellness? What are the challenges you are facing? What else comes up during your day to reflect on?

MY DAILY VIBE

"Allow your passion to become your purpose, and it will one day become your profession."

- GABRIELLE BERNSTEIN

Date: _____

(MY) WELL-BEING CHECK IN:
How I'm feeling

(MY) GRATITUDE TODAY:
What, who and things I'm grateful for

(MY) INTENTION FOR TODAY:
What I hope/intend to accomplish or even create today?

(MY) GOAL FOR WHAT I'M WORKING ON AND CREATING:

I AM:
My affirmation for today

ADDITIONAL NOTES, THOUGHTS, REFLECTIONS, VIBES AND GRATITUDE:

What are you doing to get closer to your goals, intentions, and wellness? What are the challenges you are facing? What else comes up during your day to reflect on?

MY DAILY VIBE

"Perseverance is a great element of success. If you knock long enough and loud enough at the gate, you are to wake up somebody."

- HENRY WADSWORTH LONGFELLOW

Date: _____

(MY) WELL-BEING CHECK IN:
How I'm feeling

....
....
....

(MY) GRATITUDE TODAY:
What, who and things I'm grateful for

....
....
....

(MY) INTENTION FOR TODAY:
What I hope/intend to accomplish or even create today?

....
....
....

(MY) GOAL FOR WHAT I'M WORKING ON AND CREATING:

....
....
....

I AM:
My affirmation for today

ADDITIONAL NOTES, THOUGHTS, REFLECTIONS, VIBES AND GRATITUDE:

What are you doing to get closer to your goals, intentions, and wellness? What are the challenges you are facing? What else comes up during your day to reflect on?

MY DAILY VIBE

"Allow yourself to be happy. Protect your space. Create boundaries. Decide what holds your attention. Spend time the way you choose. Give consent to yourself. It starts within. Inhale, and give yourself gratitude. Exhale and release, a smile."

— IAN DAVIS

Date: _____

(MY) WELL-BEING CHECK IN:
How I'm feeling

(MY) GRATITUDE TODAY:
What, who and things I'm grateful for

(MY) INTENTION FOR TODAY:
What I hope/intend to accomplish or even create today?

(MY) GOAL FOR WHAT I'M WORKING ON AND CREATING:

I AM:
My affirmation for today

ADDITIONAL NOTES, THOUGHTS, REFLECTIONS, VIBES AND GRATITUDE:

What are you doing to get closer to your goals, intentions, and wellness? What are the challenges you are facing? What else comes up during your day to reflect on?

MY DAILY VIBE

"Always leave people better than you found them. Hug the hurt. Kiss the broken. Befriend the lost. Love the lonely."

- MW

Date: _____

(MY) WELL-BEING CHECK IN:
How I'm feeling

....
....
....

(MY) GRATITUDE TODAY:
What, who and things I'm grateful for

....
....
....

(MY) INTENTION FOR TODAY:
What I hope/intend to accomplish or even create today?

....
....
....

(MY) GOAL FOR WHAT I'M WORKING ON AND CREATING:

....
....
....

I AM:
My affirmation for today

ADDITIONAL NOTES, THOUGHTS, REFLECTIONS, VIBES AND GRATITUDE:

What are you doing to get closer to your goals, intentions, and wellness? What are the challenges you are facing? What else comes up during your day to reflect on?

MY DAILY VIBE

"As i look back on my life, i realize that every time i thought i was being rejected from something good, i was actually being re-directed to something better."

– STEVE MARABOLI

Date: _____

❤️ (MY) WELL-BEING CHECK IN:
How I'm feeling

....
....
....

🙌 (MY) GRATITUDE TODAY:
What, who and things I'm grateful for

....
....
....

📅 (MY) INTENTION FOR TODAY:
What I hope/intend to accomplish or even create today?

....
....
....

🎯 (MY) GOAL FOR WHAT I'M WORKING ON AND CREATING:

....
....
....

💪 I AM:
My affirmation for today

ADDITIONAL NOTES, THOUGHTS, REFLECTIONS, VIBES AND GRATITUDE:

What are you doing to get closer to your goals, intentions, and wellness? What are the challenges you are facing? What else comes up during your day to reflect on?

MY DAILY VIBE

"As my sufferings mounted i soone realized that there were two ways in which I could respond... either to react with bitterness or seek to transform the suffering into a creative force."

- DR. MARTIN LUTHER KING JR.

Date: _____

(MY) WELL-BEING CHECK IN:
How I'm feeling

....
....
....

(MY) GRATITUDE TODAY:
What, who and things I'm grateful for

....
....
....

(MY) INTENTION FOR TODAY:
What I hope/intend to accomplish or even create today?

....
....
....

(MY) GOAL FOR WHAT I'M WORKING ON AND CREATING:

....
....
....

I AM:
My affirmation for today

ADDITIONAL NOTES, THOUGHTS, REFLECTIONS, VIBES AND GRATITUDE:

What are you doing to get closer to your goals, intentions, and wellness? What are the challenges you are facing? What else comes up during your day to reflect on?

MY DAILY VIBE

"As we arise each morning let us determine to respond with more love and kindness to whatever might come our way."

- THOMAS S. MONSON

Date: _____

(MY) WELL-BEING CHECK IN:
How I'm feeling

....
....
....

(MY) GRATITUDE TODAY:
What, who and things I'm grateful for

....
....
....

(MY) INTENTION FOR TODAY:
What I hope/intend to accomplish or even create today?

....
....
....

(MY) GOAL FOR WHAT I'M WORKING ON AND CREATING:

....
....
....

I AM:
My affirmation for today

ADDITIONAL NOTES, THOUGHTS, REFLECTIONS, VIBES AND GRATITUDE:

What are you doing to get closer to your goals, intentions, and wellness? What are the challenges you are facing? What else comes up during your day to reflect on?

MY DAILY VIBE

"As you think, so you shall become."
- BRUCE LEE

Date: _____

(MY) WELL-BEING CHECK IN:
How I'm feeling

....
....
....

(MY) GRATITUDE TODAY:
What, who and things I'm grateful for

....
....
....

(MY) INTENTION FOR TODAY:
What I hope/intend to accomplish or even create today?

....
....
....

(MY) GOAL FOR WHAT I'M WORKING ON AND CREATING:

....
....
....

I AM:
My affirmation for today

ADDITIONAL NOTES, THOUGHTS, REFLECTIONS, VIBES AND GRATITUDE:

What are you doing to get closer to your goals, intentions, and wellness? What are the challenges you are facing? What else comes up during your day to reflect on?

MY DAILY VIBE

"As you vibrate higher you attract more genuine people who vibrate higher too."

- LALAH DELIA

Date: _____

(MY) WELL-BEING CHECK IN:
How I'm feeling

....
....
....

(MY) GRATITUDE TODAY:
What, who and things I'm grateful for

....
....
....

(MY) INTENTION FOR TODAY:
What I hope/intend to accomplish or even create today?

....
....
....

(MY) GOAL FOR WHAT I'M WORKING ON AND CREATING:

....
....
....

I AM:
My affirmation for today

....

ADDITIONAL NOTES, THOUGHTS, REFLECTIONS, VIBES AND GRATITUDE:

What are you doing to get closer to your goals, intentions, and wellness? What are the challenges you are facing? What else comes up during your day to reflect on?

MY DAILY VIBE

"At the end of life, what really attrs is not what we bought but what we built; not what we got but what we shared; not our competence but our character; and not our success, but our significance. Live a life that matters. Live a life of love."

Date: _____

♡ (MY) WELL-BEING CHECK IN:
How I'm feeling

....
....
....

🙌 (MY) GRATITUDE TODAY:
What, who and things I'm grateful for

....
....
....

📅 (MY) INTENTION FOR TODAY:
What I hope/intend to accomplish or even create today?

....
....
....

🎯 (MY) GOAL FOR WHAT I'M WORKING ON AND CREATING:

....
....
....

💪 I AM:
My affirmation for today

ADDITIONAL NOTES, THOUGHTS, REFLECTIONS, VIBES AND GRATITUDE:

What are you doing to get closer to your goals, intentions, and wellness? What are the challenges you are facing? What else comes up during your day to reflect on?

MY DAILY VIBE

"Average people have wishes and hopes. Confident people have goals and plans."

- BRIAN TRACY

Date: _____

(MY) WELL-BEING CHECK IN:
How I'm feeling

....
....
....

(MY) GRATITUDE TODAY:
What, who and things I'm grateful for

....
....
....

(MY) INTENTION FOR TODAY:
What I hope/intend to accomplish or even create today?

....
....
....

(MY) GOAL FOR WHAT I'M WORKING ON AND CREATING:

....
....
....

I AM:
My affirmation for today

ADDITIONAL NOTES, THOUGHTS, REFLECTIONS, VIBES AND GRATITUDE:

What are you doing to get closer to your goals, intentions, and wellness? What are the challenges you are facing? What else comes up during your day to reflect on?

MY DAILY VIBE

"Be a warrior, not a worrier."

Date: _____

(MY) WELL-BEING CHECK IN:
How I'm feeling

....
....
....

(MY) GRATITUDE TODAY:
What, who and things I'm grateful for

....
....
....

(MY) INTENTION FOR TODAY:
What I hope/intend to accomplish or even create today?

....
....
....

(MY) GOAL FOR WHAT I'M WORKING ON AND CREATING:

....
....
....

I AM:
My affirmation for today

ADDITIONAL NOTES, THOUGHTS, REFLECTIONS, VIBES AND GRATITUDE:

What are you doing to get closer to your goals, intentions, and wellness? What are the challenges you are facing? What else comes up during your day to reflect on?

MY DAILY VIBE

"Be Awesome today."

Date: _____

(MY) WELL-BEING CHECK IN:
How I'm feeling

....
....
....

(MY) GRATITUDE TODAY:
What, who and things I'm grateful for

....
....
....

(MY) INTENTION FOR TODAY:
What I hope/intend to accomplish or even create today?

....
....
....

(MY) GOAL FOR WHAT I'M WORKING ON AND CREATING:

....
....
....

I AM:
My affirmation for today

ADDITIONAL NOTES, THOUGHTS, REFLECTIONS, VIBES AND GRATITUDE:

What are you doing to get closer to your goals, intentions, and wellness? What are the challenges you are facing? What else comes up during your day to reflect on?

MY DAILY VIBE

"Be brave. Even if you're not, pretend to be."
- H. JACKSON BROWN JR.

Date: _____

(MY) WELL-BEING CHECK IN:
How I'm feeling

....
....
....

(MY) GRATITUDE TODAY:
What, who and things I'm grateful for

....
....
....

(MY) INTENTION FOR TODAY:
What I hope/intend to accomplish or even create today?

....
....
....

(MY) GOAL FOR WHAT I'M WORKING ON AND CREATING:

....
....
....

I AM:
My affirmation for today

ADDITIONAL NOTES, THOUGHTS, REFLECTIONS, VIBES AND GRATITUDE:

What are you doing to get closer to your goals, intentions, and wellness? What are the challenges you are facing? What else comes up during your day to reflect on?

MY DAILY VIBE

*"Be content with what you have; rejoice in the way things are.
When you realize there is nothing lacking, the whole world belongs to you."*

- LAO TZU

Date: _____

(MY) WELL-BEING CHECK IN:
How I'm feeling

....
....
....

(MY) GRATITUDE TODAY:
What, who and things I'm grateful for

....
....
....

(MY) INTENTION FOR TODAY:
What I hope/intend to accomplish or even create today?

....
....
....

(MY) GOAL FOR WHAT I'M WORKING ON AND CREATING:

....
....
....

I AM:
My affirmation for today

....

ADDITIONAL NOTES, THOUGHTS, REFLECTIONS, VIBES AND GRATITUDE:

What are you doing to get closer to your goals, intentions, and wellness? What are the challenges you are facing? What else comes up during your day to reflect on?

MY DAILY VIBE

"Be daring, be different, be impractical; be anything that will assert integrity of purpose and imaginative vision against the play-it-safers, the creatures of the commonplace, the slaves of the ordinary."

- CECIL BEATON

Date: _____

(MY) WELL-BEING CHECK IN:
How I'm feeling

_____
_____
_____

(MY) GRATITUDE TODAY:
What, who and things I'm grateful for

_____
_____
_____

(MY) INTENTION FOR TODAY:
What I hope/intend to accomplish or even create today?

_____
_____
_____

(MY) GOAL FOR WHAT I'M WORKING ON AND CREATING:

_____
_____
_____

I AM:
My affirmation for today

ADDITIONAL NOTES, THOUGHTS, REFLECTIONS, VIBES AND GRATITUDE:

What are you doing to get closer to your goals, intentions, and wellness? What are the challenges you are facing? What else comes up during your day to reflect on?

MY DAILY VIBE

"Be happy with the little you have. There are some people with nothing who still manage to smile."

Date: _____

(MY) WELL-BEING CHECK IN:
How I'm feeling

....
....
....

(MY) GRATITUDE TODAY:
What, who and things I'm grateful for

....
....
....

(MY) INTENTION FOR TODAY:
What I hope/intend to accomplish or even create today?

....
....
....

(MY) GOAL FOR WHAT I'M WORKING ON AND CREATING:

....
....
....

I AM:
My affirmation for today

ADDITIONAL NOTES, THOUGHTS, REFLECTIONS, VIBES AND GRATITUDE:

What are you doing to get closer to your goals, intentions, and wellness? What are the challenges you are facing? What else comes up during your day to reflect on?

MY DAILY VIBE

"Be here now."

Date: _____

(MY) WELL-BEING CHECK IN:
How I'm feeling

....
....
....

(MY) GRATITUDE TODAY:
What, who and things I'm grateful for

....
....
....

(MY) INTENTION FOR TODAY:
What I hope/intend to accomplish or even create today?

....
....
....

(MY) GOAL FOR WHAT I'M WORKING ON AND CREATING:

....
....
....

I AM:
My affirmation for today

ADDITIONAL NOTES, THOUGHTS, REFLECTIONS, VIBES AND GRATITUDE:

What are you doing to get closer to your goals, intentions, and wellness? What are the challenges you are facing? What else comes up during your day to reflect on?

MY DAILY VIBE

"Be open to a work's strengths and weaknesses. As opposed to solely focusing on a weakness, allowing it to overwhelm the strengths."

- RICK RUBIN

Date: _____

(MY) WELL-BEING CHECK IN:
How I'm feeling

....
....
....

(MY) GRATITUDE TODAY:
What, who and things I'm grateful for

....
....
....

(MY) INTENTION FOR TODAY:
What I hope/intend to accomplish or even create today?

....
....
....

(MY) GOAL FOR WHAT I'M WORKING ON AND CREATING:

....
....
....

I AM:
My affirmation for today

ADDITIONAL NOTES, THOUGHTS, REFLECTIONS, VIBES AND GRATITUDE:

What are you doing to get closer to your goals, intentions, and wellness? What are the challenges you are facing? What else comes up during your day to reflect on?

MY DAILY VIBE

"Be patient. Good things will come to those who wait and continue to work hard."

Date: _____

♡ (MY) WELL-BEING CHECK IN:
How I'm feeling

....
....
....

🙌 (MY) GRATITUDE TODAY:
What, who and things I'm grateful for

....
....
....

📅 (MY) INTENTION FOR TODAY:
What I hope/intend to accomplish or even create today?

....
....
....

🎯 (MY) GOAL FOR WHAT I'M WORKING ON AND CREATING:

....
....
....

💪 I AM:
My affirmation for today

ADDITIONAL NOTES, THOUGHTS, REFLECTIONS, VIBES AND GRATITUDE:

What are you doing to get closer to your goals, intentions, and wellness? What are the challenges you are facing? What else comes up during your day to reflect on?

A FLOWER DOES NOT THINK OF COMPETING WITH THE FLOWER NEXT TO IT.
IT JUST BLOOMS

— ZEN SHIN

MY TARGETS FOR THE MONTH OF: _____

NOTES

MY DAILY VIBE

"Be so good they can't ignore you."
- STEVE MARTIN

Date: _____

(MY) WELL-BEING CHECK IN:
How I'm feeling

....
....
....

(MY) GRATITUDE TODAY:
What, who and things I'm grateful for

....
....
....

(MY) INTENTION FOR TODAY:
What I hope/intend to accomplish or even create today?

....
....
....

(MY) GOAL FOR WHAT I'M WORKING ON AND CREATING:

....
....
....

I AM:
My affirmation for today

ADDITIONAL NOTES, THOUGHTS, REFLECTIONS, VIBES AND GRATITUDE:

What are you doing to get closer to your goals, intentions, and wellness? What are the challenges you are facing? What else comes up during your day to reflect on?

MY DAILY VIBE

"Be strong, you never know who you are inspiring."

Date: _____

(MY) WELL-BEING CHECK IN:
How I'm feeling

....
....
....

(MY) GRATITUDE TODAY:
What, who and things I'm grateful for

....
....
....

(MY) INTENTION FOR TODAY:
What I hope/intend to accomplish or even create today?

....
....
....

(MY) GOAL FOR WHAT I'M WORKING ON AND CREATING:

....
....
....

I AM:
My affirmation for today

ADDITIONAL NOTES, THOUGHTS, REFLECTIONS, VIBES AND GRATITUDE:

What are you doing to get closer to your goals, intentions, and wellness? What are the challenges you are facing? What else comes up during your day to reflect on?

MY DAILY VIBE

"Being cool is being your won self, not doing something that someone else is telling you to do."

- VANESSA HUDGENS

Date: _____

(MY) WELL-BEING CHECK IN:
How I'm feeling

....
....
....

(MY) GRATITUDE TODAY:
What, who and things I'm grateful for

....
....
....

(MY) INTENTION FOR TODAY:
What I hope/intend to accomplish or even create today?

....
....
....

(MY) GOAL FOR WHAT I'M WORKING ON AND CREATING:

....
....
....

I AM:
My affirmation for today

....

ADDITIONAL NOTES, THOUGHTS, REFLECTIONS, VIBES AND GRATITUDE:

What are you doing to get closer to your goals, intentions, and wellness? What are the challenges you are facing? What else comes up during your day to reflect on?

MY DAILY VIBE

"Being defeated is often a temporary condition. Giving up is what makes it permanent."

- MARILYN VOS SAVANT

Date: _____

(MY) WELL-BEING CHECK IN:
How I'm feeling

_____
_____
_____

(MY) GRATITUDE TODAY:
What, who and things I'm grateful for

_____
_____
_____

(MY) INTENTION FOR TODAY:
What I hope/intend to accomplish or even create today?

_____
_____
_____

(MY) GOAL FOR WHAT I'M WORKING ON AND CREATING:

_____
_____
_____

I AM:
My affirmation for today

ADDITIONAL NOTES, THOUGHTS, REFLECTIONS, VIBES AND GRATITUDE:

What are you doing to get closer to your goals, intentions, and wellness? What are the challenges you are facing? What else comes up during your day to reflect on?

MY DAILY VIBE

"Belief in oneself is incredibly infectious. It generates momentum, the collective force of which far outweighs any kernel of self-doubt that may creep in."

— AIMEE MULLINS

Date: _____

(MY) WELL-BEING CHECK IN:
How I'm feeling

_____
_____
_____

(MY) GRATITUDE TODAY:
What, who and things I'm grateful for

_____
_____
_____

(MY) INTENTION FOR TODAY:
What I hope/intend to accomplish or even create today?

_____
_____
_____

(MY) GOAL FOR WHAT I'M WORKING ON AND CREATING:

_____
_____
_____

I AM:
My affirmation for today

_____

ADDITIONAL NOTES, THOUGHTS, REFLECTIONS, VIBES AND GRATITUDE:

What are you doing to get closer to your goals, intentions, and wellness? What are the challenges you are facing? What else comes up during your day to reflect on?

MY DAILY VIBE

*"Believe in yourself.
The greatest success is being yourself."*

Date: _____

(MY) WELL-BEING CHECK IN:
How I'm feeling

....
....
....

(MY) GRATITUDE TODAY:
What, who and things I'm grateful for

....
....
....

(MY) INTENTION FOR TODAY:
What I hope/intend to accomplish or even create today?

....
....
....

(MY) GOAL FOR WHAT I'M WORKING ON AND CREATING:

....
....
....

I AM:
My affirmation for today

ADDITIONAL NOTES, THOUGHTS, REFLECTIONS, VIBES AND GRATITUDE:

What are you doing to get closer to your goals, intentions, and wellness? What are the challenges you are facing? What else comes up during your day to reflect on?

MY DAILY VIBE

"Believe me, the reward is not so great without the struggle."
- WILMA RUDOLPH

Date: _____

(MY) WELL-BEING CHECK IN:
How I'm feeling

....
....
....

(MY) GRATITUDE TODAY:
What, who and things I'm grateful for

....
....
....

(MY) INTENTION FOR TODAY:
What I hope/intend to accomplish or even create today?

....
....
....

(MY) GOAL FOR WHAT I'M WORKING ON AND CREATING:

....
....
....

I AM:
My affirmation for today

....

ADDITIONAL NOTES, THOUGHTS, REFLECTIONS, VIBES AND GRATITUDE:

What are you doing to get closer to your goals, intentions, and wellness? What are the challenges you are facing? What else comes up during your day to reflect on?

MY DAILY VIBE

"Believe with all of your heart that you will do what you were made to."
- ORISON SWETT MARDEN

Date: _____

(MY) WELL-BEING CHECK IN:
How I'm feeling

....
....
....

(MY) GRATITUDE TODAY:
What, who and things I'm grateful for

....
....
....

(MY) INTENTION FOR TODAY:
What I hope/intend to accomplish or even create today?

....
....
....

(MY) GOAL FOR WHAT I'M WORKING ON AND CREATING:

....
....
....

I AM:
My affirmation for today

ADDITIONAL NOTES, THOUGHTS, REFLECTIONS, VIBES AND GRATITUDE:

What are you doing to get closer to your goals, intentions, and wellness? What are the challenges you are facing? What else comes up during your day to reflect on?

MY DAILY VIBE

"Believing that you can move mountains sometimes is more important than having the ability to do so."

— JOSHUA KUSHNER

Date: _____

(MY) WELL-BEING CHECK IN:
How I'm feeling

....
....
....

(MY) GRATITUDE TODAY:
What, who and things I'm grateful for

....
....
....

(MY) INTENTION FOR TODAY:
What I hope/intend to accomplish or even create today?

....
....
....

(MY) GOAL FOR WHAT I'M WORKING ON AND CREATING:

....
....
....

I AM:
My affirmation for today

....

ADDITIONAL NOTES, THOUGHTS, REFLECTIONS, VIBES AND GRATITUDE:

What are you doing to get closer to your goals, intentions, and wellness? What are the challenges you are facing? What else comes up during your day to reflect on?

MY DAILY VIBE

"Big shots are only little shots who keep shooting."
- CHRISTOPHER MORELY

Date: _____

♥ (MY) WELL-BEING CHECK IN:
How I'm feeling

....
....
....

🙌 (MY) GRATITUDE TODAY:
What, who and things I'm grateful for

....
....
....

📅 (MY) INTENTION FOR TODAY:
What I hope/intend to accomplish or even create today?

....
....
....

🎯 (MY) GOAL FOR WHAT I'M WORKING ON AND CREATING:

....
....
....

💪 I AM:
My affirmation for today

....

ADDITIONAL NOTES, THOUGHTS, REFLECTIONS, VIBES AND GRATITUDE:

What are you doing to get closer to your goals, intentions, and wellness? What are the challenges you are facing? What else comes up during your day to reflect on?

MY DAILY VIBE

"Breath is the bridge which connects life to consciousness, which unites your body to your thoughts. Whenever your mind becomes scattered, use your breath as the means to take hold of your mind again."

— THICH NHAT HANH

Date: _____

(MY) WELL-BEING CHECK IN:
How I'm feeling

....
....
....

(MY) GRATITUDE TODAY:
What, who and things I'm grateful for

....
....
....

(MY) INTENTION FOR TODAY:
What I hope/intend to accomplish or even create today?

....
....
....

(MY) GOAL FOR WHAT I'M WORKING ON AND CREATING:

....
....
....

I AM:
My affirmation for today

....

ADDITIONAL NOTES, THOUGHTS, REFLECTIONS, VIBES AND GRATITUDE:

What are you doing to get closer to your goals, intentions, and wellness? What are the challenges you are facing? What else comes up during your day to reflect on?

MY DAILY VIBE

"Breathe. Bring your mind back to this current moment. Any other moment, whether past or future is not occurring. Right now is what's happening. Right now is what's to be experienced."

- NICOLE ADDISON

Date: _____

(MY) WELL-BEING CHECK IN:
How I'm feeling

(MY) GRATITUDE TODAY:
What, who and things I'm grateful for

(MY) INTENTION FOR TODAY:
What I hope/intend to accomplish or even create today?

(MY) GOAL FOR WHAT I'M WORKING ON AND CREATING:

I AM:
My affirmation for today

ADDITIONAL NOTES, THOUGHTS, REFLECTIONS, VIBES AND GRATITUDE:

What are you doing to get closer to your goals, intentions, and wellness? What are the challenges you are facing? What else comes up during your day to reflect on?

MY DAILY VIBE

"But we also believe in taking risks, because that's how you move things along."

- MELINDA GATES

Date: _____

(MY) WELL-BEING CHECK IN:
How I'm feeling

....
....
....

(MY) GRATITUDE TODAY:
What, who and things I'm grateful for

....
....
....

(MY) INTENTION FOR TODAY:
What I hope/intend to accomplish or even create today?

....
....
....

(MY) GOAL FOR WHAT I'M WORKING ON AND CREATING:

....
....
....

I AM:
My affirmation for today

ADDITIONAL NOTES, THOUGHTS, REFLECTIONS, VIBES AND GRATITUDE:

What are you doing to get closer to your goals, intentions, and wellness? What are the challenges you are facing? What else comes up during your day to reflect on?

MY DAILY VIBE

"Caring about what people think of you is useless. Most people don't even know what they think of themselves."

- SONYA TECLAI

Date: _____

♥ (MY) WELL-BEING CHECK IN:
How I'm feeling

....
....
....

🙌 (MY) GRATITUDE TODAY:
What, who and things I'm grateful for

....
....
....

📅 (MY) INTENTION FOR TODAY:
What I hope/intend to accomplish or even create today?

....
....
....

🎯 (MY) GOAL FOR WHAT I'M WORKING ON AND CREATING:

....
....
....

💪 I AM:
My affirmation for today

ADDITIONAL NOTES, THOUGHTS, REFLECTIONS, VIBES AND GRATITUDE:

What are you doing to get closer to your goals, intentions, and wellness? What are the challenges you are facing? What else comes up during your day to reflect on?

MY DAILY VIBE

"Challenges are what make life interesting. Overcoming them is what makes them meaningful."

- JOSHUA J. MARINE

Date: _____

(MY) WELL-BEING CHECK IN:
How I'm feeling

....
....
....

(MY) GRATITUDE TODAY:
What, who and things I'm grateful for

....
....
....

(MY) INTENTION FOR TODAY:
What I hope/intend to accomplish or even create today?

....
....
....

(MY) GOAL FOR WHAT I'M WORKING ON AND CREATING:

....
....
....

I AM:
My affirmation for today

....

ADDITIONAL NOTES, THOUGHTS, REFLECTIONS, VIBES AND GRATITUDE:

What are you doing to get closer to your goals, intentions, and wellness? What are the challenges you are facing? What else comes up during your day to reflect on?

MY DAILY VIBE

"Change your thoughts and you change your world."
- NORMAN VINCENT PEALE

Date: _____

(MY) WELL-BEING CHECK IN:
How I'm feeling

....
....
....

(MY) GRATITUDE TODAY:
What, who and things I'm grateful for

....
....
....

(MY) INTENTION FOR TODAY:
What I hope/intend to accomplish or even create today?

....
....
....

(MY) GOAL FOR WHAT I'M WORKING ON AND CREATING:

....
....
....

I AM:
My affirmation for today

ADDITIONAL NOTES, THOUGHTS, REFLECTIONS, VIBES AND GRATITUDE:

What are you doing to get closer to your goals, intentions, and wellness? What are the challenges you are facing? What else comes up during your day to reflect on?

MY DAILY VIBE

"Choosing to be positive and having a grateful attitude is going to determine how you're going to live your life."

— JOEL OSTEEN

Date: _____

(MY) WELL-BEING CHECK IN:
How I'm feeling

....
....
....

(MY) GRATITUDE TODAY:
What, who and things I'm grateful for

....
....
....

(MY) INTENTION FOR TODAY:
What I hope/intend to accomplish or even create today?

....
....
....

(MY) GOAL FOR WHAT I'M WORKING ON AND CREATING:

....
....
....

I AM:
My affirmation for today

ADDITIONAL NOTES, THOUGHTS, REFLECTIONS, VIBES AND GRATITUDE:

What are you doing to get closer to your goals, intentions, and wellness? What are the challenges you are facing? What else comes up during your day to reflect on?

MY DAILY VIBE

"Claim your power to feel good. Feeling good is feeling god. When we feel good, we remember and recognize the god within us. May you Recognize and use the power of the words "I am". May you feel, good, abundance and fulfillment. Deep inhale, smile, exhale and release."

- IAN DAVIS

Date: _____

(MY) WELL-BEING CHECK IN:
How I'm feeling

....
....
....

(MY) GRATITUDE TODAY:
What, who and things I'm grateful for

....
....
....

(MY) INTENTION FOR TODAY:
What I hope/intend to accomplish or even create today?

....
....
....

(MY) GOAL FOR WHAT I'M WORKING ON AND CREATING:

....
....
....

I AM:
My affirmation for today

ADDITIONAL NOTES, THOUGHTS, REFLECTIONS, VIBES AND GRATITUDE:

What are you doing to get closer to your goals, intentions, and wellness? What are the challenges you are facing? What else comes up during your day to reflect on?

MY DAILY VIBE

"Clear your mind of can't."
- SAMUEL JOHNSON

Date: _____

(MY) WELL-BEING CHECK IN:
How I'm feeling

(MY) GRATITUDE TODAY:
What, who and things I'm grateful for

(MY) INTENTION FOR TODAY:
What I hope/intend to accomplish or even create today?

(MY) GOAL FOR WHAT I'M WORKING ON AND CREATING:

I AM:
My affirmation for today

ADDITIONAL NOTES, THOUGHTS, REFLECTIONS, VIBES AND GRATITUDE:

What are you doing to get closer to your goals, intentions, and wellness? What are the challenges you are facing? What else comes up during your day to reflect on?

MY DAILY VIBE

"Coming together is a beginning; keeping together is progress; working together is success."

- HENRY FORD

Date: _____

(MY) WELL-BEING CHECK IN:
How I'm feeling

....
....
....

(MY) GRATITUDE TODAY:
What, who and things I'm grateful for

....
....
....

(MY) INTENTION FOR TODAY:
What I hope/intend to accomplish or even create today?

....
....
....

(MY) GOAL FOR WHAT I'M WORKING ON AND CREATING:

....
....
....

I AM:
My affirmation for today

ADDITIONAL NOTES, THOUGHTS, REFLECTIONS, VIBES AND GRATITUDE:

What are you doing to get closer to your goals, intentions, and wellness? What are the challenges you are facing? What else comes up during your day to reflect on?

MY DAILY VIBE

"Confidence is silence. Insecurities are loud."

Date: _____

♥ (MY) WELL-BEING CHECK IN:
How I'm feeling

....
....
....

🙌 (MY) GRATITUDE TODAY:
What, who and things I'm grateful for

....
....
....

📅 (MY) INTENTION FOR TODAY:
What I hope/intend to accomplish or even create today?

....
....
....

🎯 (MY) GOAL FOR WHAT I'M WORKING ON AND CREATING:

....
....
....

💪 I AM:
My affirmation for today

ADDITIONAL NOTES, THOUGHTS, REFLECTIONS, VIBES AND GRATITUDE:

What are you doing to get closer to your goals, intentions, and wellness? What are the challenges you are facing? What else comes up during your day to reflect on?

MY DAILY VIBE

"Create! There will never be another today."
- IAN DAVIS

Date: _____

❤️ (MY) WELL-BEING CHECK IN:
How I'm feeling

....
....
....

🙌 (MY) GRATITUDE TODAY:
What, who and things I'm grateful for

....
....
....

📅 (MY) INTENTION FOR TODAY:
What I hope/intend to accomplish or even create today?

....
....
....

🎯 (MY) GOAL FOR WHAT I'M WORKING ON AND CREATING:

....
....
....

💪 I AM:
My affirmation for today

ADDITIONAL NOTES, THOUGHTS, REFLECTIONS, VIBES AND GRATITUDE:

What are you doing to get closer to your goals, intentions, and wellness? What are the challenges you are facing? What else comes up during your day to reflect on?

MY DAILY VIBE

*"Creative mind.
Creative Vibes.
Creative Life."*

Date: _____

♡ (MY) WELL-BEING CHECK IN:
How I'm feeling

....
....
....

🙌 (MY) GRATITUDE TODAY:
What, who and things I'm grateful for

....
....
....

📅 (MY) INTENTION FOR TODAY:
What I hope/intend to accomplish or even create today?

....
....
....

🎯 (MY) GOAL FOR WHAT I'M WORKING ON AND CREATING:

....
....
....

💪 I AM:
My affirmation for today

ADDITIONAL NOTES, THOUGHTS, REFLECTIONS, VIBES AND GRATITUDE:

What are you doing to get closer to your goals, intentions, and wellness? What are the challenges you are facing? What else comes up during your day to reflect on?

MY DAILY VIBE

"Creative possibilities are available to you. Each day brings new opportunities to lean toward fear or lean into love. May your day unfold with ease and grace. May you connect to the ever-present energy of love Within and around you."

— IAN DAVIS

Date: _____

(MY) WELL-BEING CHECK IN:
How I'm feeling

....
....
....

(MY) GRATITUDE TODAY:
What, who and things I'm grateful for

....
....
....

(MY) INTENTION FOR TODAY:
What I hope/intend to accomplish or even create today?

....
....
....

(MY) GOAL FOR WHAT I'M WORKING ON AND CREATING:

....
....
....

I AM:
My affirmation for today

ADDITIONAL NOTES, THOUGHTS, REFLECTIONS, VIBES AND GRATITUDE:

What are you doing to get closer to your goals, intentions, and wellness? What are the challenges you are facing? What else comes up during your day to reflect on?

MY DAILY VIBE

"Creatives hustle harder."
- IAN DAVIS

Date: _____

(MY) WELL-BEING CHECK IN:
How I'm feeling

....
....
....

(MY) GRATITUDE TODAY:
What, who and things I'm grateful for

....
....
....

(MY) INTENTION FOR TODAY:
What I hope/intend to accomplish or even create today?

....
....
....

(MY) GOAL FOR WHAT I'M WORKING ON AND CREATING:

....
....
....

I AM:
My affirmation for today

ADDITIONAL NOTES, THOUGHTS, REFLECTIONS, VIBES AND GRATITUDE:

What are you doing to get closer to your goals, intentions, and wellness? What are the challenges you are facing? What else comes up during your day to reflect on?

MY DAILY VIBE

"Discipline is just choosing between what you want now and what you want most."

— DALE PARTRIDGE

Date: _____

(MY) WELL-BEING CHECK IN:
How I'm feeling

(MY) GRATITUDE TODAY:
What, who and things I'm grateful for

(MY) INTENTION FOR TODAY:
What I hope/intend to accomplish or even create today?

(MY) GOAL FOR WHAT I'M WORKING ON AND CREATING:

I AM:
My affirmation for today

ADDITIONAL NOTES, THOUGHTS, REFLECTIONS, VIBES AND GRATITUDE:

What are you doing to get closer to your goals, intentions, and wellness? What are the challenges you are facing? What else comes up during your day to reflect on?

MY DAILY VIBE

"Do it with passion or not at all."
- ROSA NOUCHETTE CAREY

Date: _____

(MY) WELL-BEING CHECK IN:
How I'm feeling

....
....
....

(MY) GRATITUDE TODAY:
What, who and things I'm grateful for

....
....
....

(MY) INTENTION FOR TODAY:
What I hope/intend to accomplish or even create today?

....
....
....

(MY) GOAL FOR WHAT I'M WORKING ON AND CREATING:

....
....
....

I AM:
My affirmation for today

ADDITIONAL NOTES, THOUGHTS, REFLECTIONS, VIBES AND GRATITUDE:

What are you doing to get closer to your goals, intentions, and wellness? What are the challenges you are facing? What else comes up during your day to reflect on?

MY DAILY VIBE

"Do not dwell in the past, do not dream of the future, concentrate the mind on the present moment."

- HEBREWS 10:35, NIV

Date: _____

(MY) WELL-BEING CHECK IN:
How I'm feeling

....
....
....

(MY) GRATITUDE TODAY:
What, who and things I'm grateful for

....
....
....

(MY) INTENTION FOR TODAY:
What I hope/intend to accomplish or even create today?

....
....
....

(MY) GOAL FOR WHAT I'M WORKING ON AND CREATING:

....
....
....

I AM:
My affirmation for today

ADDITIONAL NOTES, THOUGHTS, REFLECTIONS, VIBES AND GRATITUDE:

What are you doing to get closer to your goals, intentions, and wellness? What are the challenges you are facing? What else comes up during your day to reflect on?

MY DAILY VIBE

"Don't allow your thoughts to be on anything you don't want."

Date: _____

(MY) WELL-BEING CHECK IN:
How I'm feeling

....
....
....

(MY) GRATITUDE TODAY:
What, who and things I'm grateful for

....
....
....

(MY) INTENTION FOR TODAY:
What I hope/intend to accomplish or even create today?

....
....
....

(MY) GOAL FOR WHAT I'M WORKING ON AND CREATING:

....
....
....

I AM:
My affirmation for today

....

ADDITIONAL NOTES, THOUGHTS, REFLECTIONS, VIBES AND GRATITUDE:

What are you doing to get closer to your goals, intentions, and wellness? What are the challenges you are facing? What else comes up during your day to reflect on?

MY DAILY VIBE

"Don't chase people. Be an example. Attract them. Work hard and be yourself. The people who belong in your life will come find you and stay. Just do your thing."

Date: _____

(MY) WELL-BEING CHECK IN:
How I'm feeling

(MY) GRATITUDE TODAY:
What, who and things I'm grateful for

(MY) INTENTION FOR TODAY:
What I hope/intend to accomplish or even create today?

(MY) GOAL FOR WHAT I'M WORKING ON AND CREATING:

I AM:
My affirmation for today

ADDITIONAL NOTES, THOUGHTS, REFLECTIONS, VIBES AND GRATITUDE:

What are you doing to get closer to your goals, intentions, and wellness? What are the challenges you are facing? What else comes up during your day to reflect on?

BE SO GOOD THEY CAN'T IGNORE YOU

- STEVE MARTIN

MY TARGETS FOR THE MONTH OF: _____

NOTES

MY DAILY VIBE

"Don't cry over the past, it's gone. Don't stress about the future, it hasn't arrived. Live in the present and make it beautiful."

Date: _____

(MY) WELL-BEING CHECK IN:
How I'm feeling

....
....
....

(MY) GRATITUDE TODAY:
What, who and things I'm grateful for

....
....
....

(MY) INTENTION FOR TODAY:
What I hope/intend to accomplish or even create today?

....
....
....

(MY) GOAL FOR WHAT I'M WORKING ON AND CREATING:

....
....
....

I AM:
My affirmation for today

ADDITIONAL NOTES, THOUGHTS, REFLECTIONS, VIBES AND GRATITUDE:

What are you doing to get closer to your goals, intentions, and wellness? What are the challenges you are facing? What else comes up during your day to reflect on?

MY DAILY VIBE

"Don't downgrade your dream just to fit your reality. Upgrader your conviction to match your destiny."

— JOHN ASSARAF

Date: _____

♡ (MY) WELL-BEING CHECK IN:
How I'm feeling

....
....
....

🙌 (MY) GRATITUDE TODAY:
What, who and things I'm grateful for

....
....
....

📅 (MY) INTENTION FOR TODAY:
What I hope/intend to accomplish or even create today?

....
....
....

🎯 (MY) GOAL FOR WHAT I'M WORKING ON AND CREATING:

....
....
....

💪 I AM:
My affirmation for today

ADDITIONAL NOTES, THOUGHTS, REFLECTIONS, VIBES AND GRATITUDE:

What are you doing to get closer to your goals, intentions, and wellness? What are the challenges you are facing? What else comes up during your day to reflect on?

MY DAILY VIBE

"Don't forget to be awesome."

Date: _____

(MY) WELL-BEING CHECK IN:
How I'm feeling

....
....
....

(MY) GRATITUDE TODAY:
What, who and things I'm grateful for

....
....
....

(MY) INTENTION FOR TODAY:
What I hope/intend to accomplish or even create today?

....
....
....

(MY) GOAL FOR WHAT I'M WORKING ON AND CREATING:

....
....
....

I AM:
My affirmation for today

ADDITIONAL NOTES, THOUGHTS, REFLECTIONS, VIBES AND GRATITUDE:

What are you doing to get closer to your goals, intentions, and wellness? What are the challenges you are facing? What else comes up during your day to reflect on?

MY DAILY VIBE

"Don't judge each day by the harvest you reap but by the seeds that you plant."

- ROBERT LOUIS STEVENSON

Date: _____

(MY) WELL-BEING CHECK IN:
How I'm feeling

....
....
....

(MY) GRATITUDE TODAY:
What, who and things I'm grateful for

....
....
....

(MY) INTENTION FOR TODAY:
What I hope/intend to accomplish or even create today?

....
....
....

(MY) GOAL FOR WHAT I'M WORKING ON AND CREATING:

....
....
....

I AM:
My affirmation for today

....

ADDITIONAL NOTES, THOUGHTS, REFLECTIONS, VIBES AND GRATITUDE:

What are you doing to get closer to your goals, intentions, and wellness? What are the challenges you are facing? What else comes up during your day to reflect on?

MY DAILY VIBE

"Don't make a habit of choosing what feels good over what is actually good for you."

– ERIC THOMAS

Date: _____

(MY) WELL-BEING CHECK IN:
How I'm feeling

....
....
....

(MY) GRATITUDE TODAY:
What, who and things I'm grateful for

....
....
....

(MY) INTENTION FOR TODAY:
What I hope/intend to accomplish or even create today?

....
....
....

(MY) GOAL FOR WHAT I'M WORKING ON AND CREATING:

....
....
....

I AM:
My affirmation for today

ADDITIONAL NOTES, THOUGHTS, REFLECTIONS, VIBES AND GRATITUDE:

What are you doing to get closer to your goals, intentions, and wellness? What are the challenges you are facing? What else comes up during your day to reflect on?

MY DAILY VIBE

"Don't quit"

Date: _____

(MY) WELL-BEING CHECK IN:
How I'm feeling

....
....
....

(MY) GRATITUDE TODAY:
What, who and things I'm grateful for

....
....
....

(MY) INTENTION FOR TODAY:
What I hope/intend to accomplish or even create today?

....
....
....

(MY) GOAL FOR WHAT I'M WORKING ON AND CREATING:

....
....
....

I AM:
My affirmation for today

ADDITIONAL NOTES, THOUGHTS, REFLECTIONS, VIBES AND GRATITUDE:

What are you doing to get closer to your goals, intentions, and wellness? What are the challenges you are facing? What else comes up during your day to reflect on?

MY DAILY VIBE

"Don't raise your voice. improve your argument."
- DESMOND TUTU

Date: _____

(MY) WELL-BEING CHECK IN:
How I'm feeling

....
....
....

(MY) GRATITUDE TODAY:
What, who and things I'm grateful for

....
....
....

(MY) INTENTION FOR TODAY:
What I hope/intend to accomplish or even create today?

....
....
....

(MY) GOAL FOR WHAT I'M WORKING ON AND CREATING:

....
....
....

I AM:
My affirmation for today

ADDITIONAL NOTES, THOUGHTS, REFLECTIONS, VIBES AND GRATITUDE:

What are you doing to get closer to your goals, intentions, and wellness? What are the challenges you are facing? What else comes up during your day to reflect on?

MY DAILY VIBE

"Don't talk fear, talk faith!"

Date: _____

❤️ (MY) WELL-BEING CHECK IN:
How I'm feeling

....
....
....

🙌 (MY) GRATITUDE TODAY:
What, who and things I'm grateful for

....
....
....

📅 (MY) INTENTION FOR TODAY:
What I hope/intend to accomplish or even create today?

....
....
....

🎯 (MY) GOAL FOR WHAT I'M WORKING ON AND CREATING:

....
....
....

💪 I AM:
My affirmation for today

ADDITIONAL NOTES, THOUGHTS, REFLECTIONS, VIBES AND GRATITUDE:

What are you doing to get closer to your goals, intentions, and wellness? What are the challenges you are facing? What else comes up during your day to reflect on?

MY DAILY VIBE

"Don't tell people your dreams. Show them."

Date: _____

(MY) WELL-BEING CHECK IN:
How I'm feeling

....
....
....

(MY) GRATITUDE TODAY:
What, who and things I'm grateful for

....
....
....

(MY) INTENTION FOR TODAY:
What I hope/intend to accomplish or even create today?

....
....
....

(MY) GOAL FOR WHAT I'M WORKING ON AND CREATING:

....
....
....

I AM:
My affirmation for today

....

ADDITIONAL NOTES, THOUGHTS, REFLECTIONS, VIBES AND GRATITUDE:

What are you doing to get closer to your goals, intentions, and wellness? What are the challenges you are facing? What else comes up during your day to reflect on?

MY DAILY VIBE

"Don't wait for it to happen, go make it happen."

Date: _____

❤️ (MY) WELL-BEING CHECK IN:
How I'm feeling

....

....

....

🙌 (MY) GRATITUDE TODAY:
What, who and things I'm grateful for

....

....

....

📅 (MY) INTENTION FOR TODAY:
What I hope/intend to accomplish or even create today?

....

....

....

🎯 (MY) GOAL FOR WHAT I'M WORKING ON AND CREATING:

....

....

....

💪 I AM:
My affirmation for today

....

ADDITIONAL NOTES, THOUGHTS, REFLECTIONS, VIBES AND GRATITUDE:

What are you doing to get closer to your goals, intentions, and wellness? What are the challenges you are facing? What else comes up during your day to reflect on?

MY DAILY VIBE

"Don't wait for the right opportunity. Create it."
- GEORGE BERNARD SHAW

Date: _____

(MY) WELL-BEING CHECK IN:
How I'm feeling

....
....
....

(MY) GRATITUDE TODAY:
What, who and things I'm grateful for

....
....
....

(MY) INTENTION FOR TODAY:
What I hope/intend to accomplish or even create today?

....
....
....

(MY) GOAL FOR WHAT I'M WORKING ON AND CREATING:

....
....
....

I AM:
My affirmation for today

ADDITIONAL NOTES, THOUGHTS, REFLECTIONS, VIBES AND GRATITUDE:

What are you doing to get closer to your goals, intentions, and wellness? What are the challenges you are facing? What else comes up during your day to reflect on?

MY DAILY VIBE

"Don't wait. The time will never be just right."
- NAPOLEON HILL

Date: _____

(MY) WELL-BEING CHECK IN:
How I'm feeling

....
....
....

(MY) GRATITUDE TODAY:
What, who and things I'm grateful for

....
....
....

(MY) INTENTION FOR TODAY:
What I hope/intend to accomplish or even create today?

....
....
....

(MY) GOAL FOR WHAT I'M WORKING ON AND CREATING:

....
....
....

I AM:
My affirmation for today

ADDITIONAL NOTES, THOUGHTS, REFLECTIONS, VIBES AND GRATITUDE:

What are you doing to get closer to your goals, intentions, and wellness? What are the challenges you are facing? What else comes up during your day to reflect on?

MY DAILY VIBE

"Don't wish for it work for it."

Date: _____

♥ (MY) WELL-BEING CHECK IN:
How I'm feeling

....
....
....

🙌 (MY) GRATITUDE TODAY:
What, who and things I'm grateful for

....
....
....

📅 (MY) INTENTION FOR TODAY:
What I hope/intend to accomplish or even create today?

....
....
....

🎯 (MY) GOAL FOR WHAT I'M WORKING ON AND CREATING:

....
....
....

💪 I AM:
My affirmation for today

ADDITIONAL NOTES, THOUGHTS, REFLECTIONS, VIBES AND GRATITUDE:

What are you doing to get closer to your goals, intentions, and wellness? What are the challenges you are facing? What else comes up during your day to reflect on?

MY DAILY VIBE

"Don't worry about the future or worry, but know that worrying is as effective as trying to solve an algebra equation by chewing bubble gum."

- BAZ LUHRMANN

Date: _____

(MY) WELL-BEING CHECK IN:
How I'm feeling

....
....
....

(MY) GRATITUDE TODAY:
What, who and things I'm grateful for

....
....
....

(MY) INTENTION FOR TODAY:
What I hope/intend to accomplish or even create today?

....
....
....

(MY) GOAL FOR WHAT I'M WORKING ON AND CREATING:

....
....
....

I AM:
My affirmation for today

ADDITIONAL NOTES, THOUGHTS, REFLECTIONS, VIBES AND GRATITUDE:

What are you doing to get closer to your goals, intentions, and wellness? What are the challenges you are facing? What else comes up during your day to reflect on?

MY DAILY VIBE

"Dream big, work hard, stay focused and surround yourself with good people."

Date: _____

❤️ (MY) WELL-BEING CHECK IN:
How I'm feeling

....

....

....

🙌 (MY) GRATITUDE TODAY:
What, who and things I'm grateful for

....

....

....

📅 (MY) INTENTION FOR TODAY:
What I hope/intend to accomplish or even create today?

....

....

....

🎯 (MY) GOAL FOR WHAT I'M WORKING ON AND CREATING:

....

....

....

💪 I AM:
My affirmation for today

ADDITIONAL NOTES, THOUGHTS, REFLECTIONS, VIBES AND GRATITUDE:

What are you doing to get closer to your goals, intentions, and wellness? What are the challenges you are facing? What else comes up during your day to reflect on?

MY DAILY VIBE

"Dreams don't work unless you do."
- JOHN C. MAXWELL

Date: _____

(MY) WELL-BEING CHECK IN:
How I'm feeling

....
....
....

(MY) GRATITUDE TODAY:
What, who and things I'm grateful for

....
....
....

(MY) INTENTION FOR TODAY:
What I hope/intend to accomplish or even create today?

....
....
....

(MY) GOAL FOR WHAT I'M WORKING ON AND CREATING:

....
....
....

I AM:
My affirmation for today

....

ADDITIONAL NOTES, THOUGHTS, REFLECTIONS, VIBES AND GRATITUDE:

What are you doing to get closer to your goals, intentions, and wellness? What are the challenges you are facing? What else comes up during your day to reflect on?

MY DAILY VIBE

"Each day is a fresh start with a clean slate. The past is gone and the future isn't here yet – own the now. May you Give yourself permission to feel good,– To be aware, abundant, fulfilled and be your best."

– IAN DAVIS

Date: _____

(MY) WELL-BEING CHECK IN:
How I'm feeling

....
....
....

(MY) GRATITUDE TODAY:
What, who and things I'm grateful for

....
....
....

(MY) INTENTION FOR TODAY:
What I hope/intend to accomplish or even create today?

....
....
....

(MY) GOAL FOR WHAT I'M WORKING ON AND CREATING:

....
....
....

I AM:
My affirmation for today

ADDITIONAL NOTES, THOUGHTS, REFLECTIONS, VIBES AND GRATITUDE:

What are you doing to get closer to your goals, intentions, and wellness? What are the challenges you are facing? What else comes up during your day to reflect on?

MY DAILY VIBE

"Each day is a new birth unlimited with miraculous possibilities. May your thinking be clear with purpose. May your heart be free to love. May you free your mind from all limitation and lack. May you embody the energy of love."

— IAN DAVIS

Date: _____

(MY) WELL-BEING CHECK IN:
How I'm feeling

(MY) GRATITUDE TODAY:
What, who and things I'm grateful for

(MY) INTENTION FOR TODAY:
What I hope/intend to accomplish or even create today?

(MY) GOAL FOR WHAT I'M WORKING ON AND CREATING:

I AM:
My affirmation for today

ADDITIONAL NOTES, THOUGHTS, REFLECTIONS, VIBES AND GRATITUDE:

What are you doing to get closer to your goals, intentions, and wellness? What are the challenges you are facing? What else comes up during your day to reflect on?

MY DAILY VIBE

"Ego Says: "Once everything falls into place, I'll feel peace."
Spirits says: "Find your peace, and then everything will fall into place."."

— MARIANNE WILLIAMSON

Date: _____

(MY) WELL-BEING CHECK IN:
How I'm feeling

....
....
....

(MY) GRATITUDE TODAY:
What, who and things I'm grateful for

....
....
....

(MY) INTENTION FOR TODAY:
What I hope/intend to accomplish or even create today?

....
....
....

(MY) GOAL FOR WHAT I'M WORKING ON AND CREATING:

....
....
....

I AM:
My affirmation for today

ADDITIONAL NOTES, THOUGHTS, REFLECTIONS, VIBES AND GRATITUDE:

What are you doing to get closer to your goals, intentions, and wellness? What are the challenges you are facing? What else comes up during your day to reflect on?

MY DAILY VIBE

"Either I will find a way, or i will make one."
- PHILIP SIDNEY

Date: _____

♥ (MY) WELL-BEING CHECK IN:
How I'm feeling

....
....
....

🙌 (MY) GRATITUDE TODAY:
What, who and things I'm grateful for

....
....
....

📅 (MY) INTENTION FOR TODAY:
What I hope/intend to accomplish or even create today?

....
....
....

🎯 (MY) GOAL FOR WHAT I'M WORKING ON AND CREATING:

....
....
....

💪 I AM:
My affirmation for today

ADDITIONAL NOTES, THOUGHTS, REFLECTIONS, VIBES AND GRATITUDE:

What are you doing to get closer to your goals, intentions, and wellness? What are the challenges you are facing? What else comes up during your day to reflect on?

MY DAILY VIBE

"Either you run the day, or the day runs you."
- JIM ROHN

Date: _____

(MY) WELL-BEING CHECK IN:
How I'm feeling

(MY) GRATITUDE TODAY:
What, who and things I'm grateful for

(MY) INTENTION FOR TODAY:
What I hope/intend to accomplish or even create today?

(MY) GOAL FOR WHAT I'M WORKING ON AND CREATING:

I AM:
My affirmation for today

ADDITIONAL NOTES, THOUGHTS, REFLECTIONS, VIBES AND GRATITUDE:

What are you doing to get closer to your goals, intentions, and wellness? What are the challenges you are facing? What else comes up during your day to reflect on?

MY DAILY VIBE

"Energy, like the bibilial grain of mustard see, will move mountains."
- HOSEA BALLOU

Date: _____

❤️ (MY) WELL-BEING CHECK IN:
How I'm feeling

....
....
....

🙌 (MY) GRATITUDE TODAY:
What, who and things I'm grateful for

....
....
....

📅 (MY) INTENTION FOR TODAY:
What I hope/intend to accomplish or even create today?

....
....
....

🎯 (MY) GOAL FOR WHAT I'M WORKING ON AND CREATING:

....
....
....

💪 I AM:
My affirmation for today

ADDITIONAL NOTES, THOUGHTS, REFLECTIONS, VIBES AND GRATITUDE:

What are you doing to get closer to your goals, intentions, and wellness? What are the challenges you are facing? What else comes up during your day to reflect on?

MY DAILY VIBE

"Every artist was once an amateur."
- RALPH WALDO EMERSON

Date: _____

❤️ (MY) WELL-BEING CHECK IN:
How I'm feeling

....
....
....

🙌 (MY) GRATITUDE TODAY:
What, who and things I'm grateful for

....
....
....

📅 (MY) INTENTION FOR TODAY:
What I hope/intend to accomplish or even create today?

....
....
....

🎯 (MY) GOAL FOR WHAT I'M WORKING ON AND CREATING:

....
....
....

💪 I AM:
My affirmation for today

ADDITIONAL NOTES, THOUGHTS, REFLECTIONS, VIBES AND GRATITUDE:

What are you doing to get closer to your goals, intentions, and wellness? What are the challenges you are facing? What else comes up during your day to reflect on?

MY DAILY VIBE

"Every word you speak and every thought you think is an affirmation for your future."

- CHERYL RICHARDSON

Date: _____

(MY) WELL-BEING CHECK IN:
How I'm feeling

....

....

....

(MY) GRATITUDE TODAY:
What, who and things I'm grateful for

....

....

....

(MY) INTENTION FOR TODAY:
What I hope/intend to accomplish or even create today?

....

....

....

(MY) GOAL FOR WHAT I'M WORKING ON AND CREATING:

....

....

....

I AM:
My affirmation for today

....

ADDITIONAL NOTES, THOUGHTS, REFLECTIONS, VIBES AND GRATITUDE:

What are you doing to get closer to your goals, intentions, and wellness? What are the challenges you are facing? What else comes up during your day to reflect on?

MY DAILY VIBE

"Everyone you meet is fighting a battle you know nothing about. be kind. Always."

- BRAD MELTZER

Date: _____

(MY) WELL-BEING CHECK IN:
How I'm feeling

....
....
....

(MY) GRATITUDE TODAY:
What, who and things I'm grateful for

....
....
....

(MY) INTENTION FOR TODAY:
What I hope/intend to accomplish or even create today?

....
....
....

(MY) GOAL FOR WHAT I'M WORKING ON AND CREATING:

....
....
....

I AM:
My affirmation for today

ADDITIONAL NOTES, THOUGHTS, REFLECTIONS, VIBES AND GRATITUDE:

What are you doing to get closer to your goals, intentions, and wellness? What are the challenges you are facing? What else comes up during your day to reflect on?

MY DAILY VIBE

"Everything in the universe is within you. Ask all from yourself."
- RUMI

Date: _____

(MY) WELL-BEING CHECK IN:
How I'm feeling

....
....
....

(MY) GRATITUDE TODAY:
What, who and things I'm grateful for

....
....
....

(MY) INTENTION FOR TODAY:
What I hope/intend to accomplish or even create today?

....
....
....

(MY) GOAL FOR WHAT I'M WORKING ON AND CREATING:

....
....
....

I AM:
My affirmation for today

....

ADDITIONAL NOTES, THOUGHTS, REFLECTIONS, VIBES AND GRATITUDE:

What are you doing to get closer to your goals, intentions, and wellness? What are the challenges you are facing? What else comes up during your day to reflect on?

MY DAILY VIBE

"Excellence is my presence, never tense, never hesitant."
- NOTORIOUS BIG

Date: _____

(MY) WELL-BEING CHECK IN:
How I'm feeling

....
....
....

(MY) GRATITUDE TODAY:
What, who and things I'm grateful for

....
....
....

(MY) INTENTION FOR TODAY:
What I hope/intend to accomplish or even create today?

....
....
....

(MY) GOAL FOR WHAT I'M WORKING ON AND CREATING:

....
....
....

I AM:
My affirmation for today

ADDITIONAL NOTES, THOUGHTS, REFLECTIONS, VIBES AND GRATITUDE:

What are you doing to get closer to your goals, intentions, and wellness? What are the challenges you are facing? What else comes up during your day to reflect on?

MY DAILY VIBE

"Excellence is never an accident; it is the result of high intention, sincere effort, intelligent direction, skillful execution and the vision to see obstacles as opportunities."

- ANONYMOUS

Date: _____

(MY) WELL-BEING CHECK IN:
How I'm feeling

(MY) GRATITUDE TODAY:
What, who and things I'm grateful for

(MY) INTENTION FOR TODAY:
What I hope/intend to accomplish or even create today?

(MY) GOAL FOR WHAT I'M WORKING ON AND CREATING:

I AM:
My affirmation for today

ADDITIONAL NOTES, THOUGHTS, REFLECTIONS, VIBES AND GRATITUDE:

What are you doing to get closer to your goals, intentions, and wellness? What are the challenges you are facing? What else comes up during your day to reflect on?

MY DAILY VIBE

"Faith is taking the first step even when you don't see the whole staircase."
- DR. MARTIN LUTHER KING JR.

Date: _____

(MY) WELL-BEING CHECK IN:
How I'm feeling

_____
_____
_____

(MY) GRATITUDE TODAY:
What, who and things I'm grateful for

_____
_____
_____

(MY) INTENTION FOR TODAY:
What I hope/intend to accomplish or even create today?

_____
_____
_____

(MY) GOAL FOR WHAT I'M WORKING ON AND CREATING:

_____
_____
_____

I AM:
My affirmation for today

ADDITIONAL NOTES, THOUGHTS, REFLECTIONS, VIBES AND GRATITUDE:

What are you doing to get closer to your goals, intentions, and wellness? What are the challenges you are facing? What else comes up during your day to reflect on?

MY DAILY VIBE

"Figure out your weakness and don't make it your weakness anymore."
-STACEY LEWIS

Date: _____

(MY) WELL-BEING CHECK IN:
How I'm feeling

....
....
....

(MY) GRATITUDE TODAY:
What, who and things I'm grateful for

....
....
....

(MY) INTENTION FOR TODAY:
What I hope/intend to accomplish or even create today?

....
....
....

(MY) GOAL FOR WHAT I'M WORKING ON AND CREATING:

....
....
....

I AM:
My affirmation for today

ADDITIONAL NOTES, THOUGHTS, REFLECTIONS, VIBES AND GRATITUDE:

What are you doing to get closer to your goals, intentions, and wellness? What are the challenges you are facing? What else comes up during your day to reflect on?

RISK vs REWARD IS THE NEW ROI.

- REBEKAH GRIPPA

MY TARGETS FOR THE MONTH OF: _____

NOTES

MY DAILY VIBE

"Focus on making yourself better, not on thinking that you are better."

Date: _____

♡ (MY) WELL-BEING CHECK IN:
How I'm feeling

....
....
....

🙌 (MY) GRATITUDE TODAY:
What, who and things I'm grateful for

....
....
....

📅 (MY) INTENTION FOR TODAY:
What I hope/intend to accomplish or even create today?

....
....
....

🎯 (MY) GOAL FOR WHAT I'M WORKING ON AND CREATING:

....
....
....

💪 I AM:
My affirmation for today

ADDITIONAL NOTES, THOUGHTS, REFLECTIONS, VIBES AND GRATITUDE:

What are you doing to get closer to your goals, intentions, and wellness? What are the challenges you are facing? What else comes up during your day to reflect on?

MY DAILY VIBE

"Forget past mistakes. Forget Failures. Forget everything except what you're going to do now and do it."

— WILL DURANT

Date: _____

♡ (MY) WELL-BEING CHECK IN:
How I'm feeling

_____
_____
_____

🙌 (MY) GRATITUDE TODAY:
What, who and things I'm grateful for

_____
_____
_____

📅 (MY) INTENTION FOR TODAY:
What I hope/intend to accomplish or even create today?

_____
_____
_____

🎯 (MY) GOAL FOR WHAT I'M WORKING ON AND CREATING:

_____
_____
_____

💪 I AM:
My affirmation for today

ADDITIONAL NOTES, THOUGHTS, REFLECTIONS, VIBES AND GRATITUDE:

What are you doing to get closer to your goals, intentions, and wellness? What are the challenges you are facing? What else comes up during your day to reflect on?

MY DAILY VIBE

"Give thanks for your creativity."

Date: _____

(MY) WELL-BEING CHECK IN:
How I'm feeling

....
....
....

(MY) GRATITUDE TODAY:
What, who and things I'm grateful for

....
....
....

(MY) INTENTION FOR TODAY:
What I hope/intend to accomplish or even create today?

....
....
....

(MY) GOAL FOR WHAT I'M WORKING ON AND CREATING:

....
....
....

I AM:
My affirmation for today

....

ADDITIONAL NOTES, THOUGHTS, REFLECTIONS, VIBES AND GRATITUDE:

What are you doing to get closer to your goals, intentions, and wellness? What are the challenges you are facing? What else comes up during your day to reflect on?

MY DAILY VIBE

"Give yourself permission. Don't place limits on your thinking. Recognize and notice what you say. How do your words affect you and other people? Choose words that uplift and lead you on the right path. May you have an abundant day and week!"

- IAN DAVIS

Date: _____

(MY) WELL-BEING CHECK IN:
How I'm feeling

_____
_____
_____

(MY) GRATITUDE TODAY:
What, who and things I'm grateful for

_____
_____
_____

(MY) INTENTION FOR TODAY:
What I hope/intend to accomplish or even create today?

_____
_____
_____

(MY) GOAL FOR WHAT I'M WORKING ON AND CREATING:

_____
_____
_____

I AM:
My affirmation for today

ADDITIONAL NOTES, THOUGHTS, REFLECTIONS, VIBES AND GRATITUDE:

What are you doing to get closer to your goals, intentions, and wellness? What are the challenges you are facing? What else comes up during your day to reflect on?

MY DAILY VIBE

"Giving up on your goal because of one setback is like slashing your other three tires because you got a flat."

- CHRIS GARDNER

Date: _____

(MY) WELL-BEING CHECK IN:
How I'm feeling

(MY) GRATITUDE TODAY:
What, who and things I'm grateful for

(MY) INTENTION FOR TODAY:
What I hope/intend to accomplish or even create today?

(MY) GOAL FOR WHAT I'M WORKING ON AND CREATING:

I AM:
My affirmation for today

ADDITIONAL NOTES, THOUGHTS, REFLECTIONS, VIBES AND GRATITUDE:

What are you doing to get closer to your goals, intentions, and wellness? What are the challenges you are facing? What else comes up during your day to reflect on?

MY DAILY VIBE

"Go ahead. You never know what could be on the other side."
- ANONYMOUSR

Date: _____

♥ (MY) WELL-BEING CHECK IN:
How I'm feeling

....
....
....

🙌 (MY) GRATITUDE TODAY:
What, who and things I'm grateful for

....
....
....

📅 (MY) INTENTION FOR TODAY:
What I hope/intend to accomplish or even create today?

....
....
....

🎯 (MY) GOAL FOR WHAT I'M WORKING ON AND CREATING:

....
....
....

💪 I AM:
My affirmation for today

ADDITIONAL NOTES, THOUGHTS, REFLECTIONS, VIBES AND GRATITUDE:

What are you doing to get closer to your goals, intentions, and wellness? What are the challenges you are facing? What else comes up during your day to reflect on?

MY DAILY VIBE

"Go big or go home."

Date: _____

❤️ (MY) WELL-BEING CHECK IN:
How I'm feeling

....
....
....

🙌 (MY) GRATITUDE TODAY:
What, who and things I'm grateful for

....
....
....

📅 (MY) INTENTION FOR TODAY:
What I hope/intend to accomplish or even create today?

....
....
....

🎯 (MY) GOAL FOR WHAT I'M WORKING ON AND CREATING:

....
....
....

💪 I AM:
My affirmation for today

ADDITIONAL NOTES, THOUGHTS, REFLECTIONS, VIBES AND GRATITUDE:

What are you doing to get closer to your goals, intentions, and wellness? What are the challenges you are facing? What else comes up during your day to reflect on?

MY DAILY VIBE

"Go confidently in the direction of your dreams. Live the life you have imagined."

- HENRY DAVID THOREAU

Date: _____

(MY) WELL-BEING CHECK IN:
How I'm feeling

_____
_____
_____

(MY) GRATITUDE TODAY:
What, who and things I'm grateful for

_____
_____
_____

(MY) INTENTION FOR TODAY:
What I hope/intend to accomplish or even create today?

_____
_____
_____

(MY) GOAL FOR WHAT I'M WORKING ON AND CREATING:

_____
_____
_____

I AM:
My affirmation for today

ADDITIONAL NOTES, THOUGHTS, REFLECTIONS, VIBES AND GRATITUDE:

What are you doing to get closer to your goals, intentions, and wellness? What are the challenges you are facing? What else comes up during your day to reflect on?

MY DAILY VIBE

"Go for now. The future is promised to no one."
- WAYNE DYER

Date: _____

(MY) WELL-BEING CHECK IN:
How I'm feeling

....
....
....

(MY) GRATITUDE TODAY:
What, who and things I'm grateful for

....
....
....

(MY) INTENTION FOR TODAY:
What I hope/intend to accomplish or even create today?

....
....
....

(MY) GOAL FOR WHAT I'M WORKING ON AND CREATING:

....
....
....

I AM:
My affirmation for today

ADDITIONAL NOTES, THOUGHTS, REFLECTIONS, VIBES AND GRATITUDE:

What are you doing to get closer to your goals, intentions, and wellness? What are the challenges you are facing? What else comes up during your day to reflect on?

MY DAILY VIBE

"Good things happen to those who hustle."

Date: _____

❤️ (MY) WELL-BEING CHECK IN:
How I'm feeling

_____
_____
_____

🙌 (MY) GRATITUDE TODAY:
What, who and things I'm grateful for

_____
_____
_____

📅 (MY) INTENTION FOR TODAY:
What I hope/intend to accomplish or even create today?

_____
_____
_____

🎯 (MY) GOAL FOR WHAT I'M WORKING ON AND CREATING:

_____
_____
_____

💪 I AM:
My affirmation for today

ADDITIONAL NOTES, THOUGHTS, REFLECTIONS, VIBES AND GRATITUDE:

What are you doing to get closer to your goals, intentions, and wellness? What are the challenges you are facing? What else comes up during your day to reflect on?

MY DAILY VIBE

*"Good, better, best.
Never let it rest.
'Til your good is better and your better best."*

- ST. JEROME

Date: _____

(MY) WELL-BEING CHECK IN:
How I'm feeling

....
....
....

(MY) GRATITUDE TODAY:
What, who and things I'm grateful for

....
....
....

(MY) INTENTION FOR TODAY:
What I hope/intend to accomplish or even create today?

....
....
....

(MY) GOAL FOR WHAT I'M WORKING ON AND CREATING:

....
....
....

I AM:
My affirmation for today

ADDITIONAL NOTES, THOUGHTS, REFLECTIONS, VIBES AND GRATITUDE:

What are you doing to get closer to your goals, intentions, and wellness? What are the challenges you are facing? What else comes up during your day to reflect on?

MY DAILY VIBE

"Great minds discuss ideas, average minds discuss events, small minds discuss people."
- ELEANOR ROOSEVELT

Date: _____

(MY) WELL-BEING CHECK IN:
How I'm feeling

_____
_____
_____

(MY) GRATITUDE TODAY:
What, who and things I'm grateful for

_____
_____
_____

(MY) INTENTION FOR TODAY:
What I hope/intend to accomplish or even create today?

_____
_____
_____

(MY) GOAL FOR WHAT I'M WORKING ON AND CREATING:

_____
_____
_____

I AM:
My affirmation for today

ADDITIONAL NOTES, THOUGHTS, REFLECTIONS, VIBES AND GRATITUDE:

What are you doing to get closer to your goals, intentions, and wellness? What are the challenges you are facing? What else comes up during your day to reflect on?

MY DAILY VIBE

"Grit is sticking with your future day in, day out and not just for the week, not just for the month, but for years."

- ANGELA DUCKWORTH

Date: _____

(MY) WELL-BEING CHECK IN:
How I'm feeling

(MY) GRATITUDE TODAY:
What, who and things I'm grateful for

(MY) INTENTION FOR TODAY:
What I hope/intend to accomplish or even create today?

(MY) GOAL FOR WHAT I'M WORKING ON AND CREATING:

I AM:
My affirmation for today

ADDITIONAL NOTES, THOUGHTS, REFLECTIONS, VIBES AND GRATITUDE:

What are you doing to get closer to your goals, intentions, and wellness? What are the challenges you are facing? What else comes up during your day to reflect on?

MY DAILY VIBE

"Growth is painful. Change is painful. But nothing is as painful as staying stuck somewhere you don't belong."

— MANDY HALE

Date: _____

(MY) WELL-BEING CHECK IN:
How I'm feeling

(MY) GRATITUDE TODAY:
What, who and things I'm grateful for

(MY) INTENTION FOR TODAY:
What I hope/intend to accomplish or even create today?

(MY) GOAL FOR WHAT I'M WORKING ON AND CREATING:

I AM:
My affirmation for today

ADDITIONAL NOTES, THOUGHTS, REFLECTIONS, VIBES AND GRATITUDE:

What are you doing to get closer to your goals, intentions, and wellness? What are the challenges you are facing? What else comes up during your day to reflect on?

MY DAILY VIBE

"Happiness is not something readymade. It comes from our own actions."
- DALAI LAMA

Date: _____

♥ (MY) WELL-BEING CHECK IN:
How I'm feeling

....
....
....

🙌 (MY) GRATITUDE TODAY:
What, who and things I'm grateful for

....
....
....

📅 (MY) INTENTION FOR TODAY:
What I hope/intend to accomplish or even create today?

....
....
....

🎯 (MY) GOAL FOR WHAT I'M WORKING ON AND CREATING:

....
....
....

💪 I AM:
My affirmation for today

....

ADDITIONAL NOTES, THOUGHTS, REFLECTIONS, VIBES AND GRATITUDE:

What are you doing to get closer to your goals, intentions, and wellness? What are the challenges you are facing? What else comes up during your day to reflect on?

MY DAILY VIBE

"Happiness is the real rich. Health is the real wealth. Kindness is the real cool. And a peace of mind is the real bag."

Date: _____

(MY) WELL-BEING CHECK IN:
How I'm feeling

(MY) GRATITUDE TODAY:
What, who and things I'm grateful for

(MY) INTENTION FOR TODAY:
What I hope/intend to accomplish or even create today?

(MY) GOAL FOR WHAT I'M WORKING ON AND CREATING:

I AM:
My affirmation for today

ADDITIONAL NOTES, THOUGHTS, REFLECTIONS, VIBES AND GRATITUDE:

What are you doing to get closer to your goals, intentions, and wellness? What are the challenges you are facing? What else comes up during your day to reflect on?

MY DAILY VIBE

"Hard work will always overcome natural talent when natural talent does not work hard enough."

- SIR ALEX FERGUSON

Date: _____

(MY) WELL-BEING CHECK IN:
How I'm feeling

(MY) GRATITUDE TODAY:
What, who and things I'm grateful for

(MY) INTENTION FOR TODAY:
What I hope/intend to accomplish or even create today?

(MY) GOAL FOR WHAT I'M WORKING ON AND CREATING:

I AM:
My affirmation for today

ADDITIONAL NOTES, THOUGHTS, REFLECTIONS, VIBES AND GRATITUDE:

What are you doing to get closer to your goals, intentions, and wellness? What are the challenges you are facing? What else comes up during your day to reflect on?

MY DAILY VIBE

"Hardships often prepare ordinary people for an extraordinary destiny."
- C.S. LEWIS

Date: _____

(MY) WELL-BEING CHECK IN:
How I'm feeling

....
....
....

(MY) GRATITUDE TODAY:
What, who and things I'm grateful for

....
....
....

(MY) INTENTION FOR TODAY:
What I hope/intend to accomplish or even create today?

....
....
....

(MY) GOAL FOR WHAT I'M WORKING ON AND CREATING:

....
....
....

I AM:
My affirmation for today

ADDITIONAL NOTES, THOUGHTS, REFLECTIONS, VIBES AND GRATITUDE:

What are you doing to get closer to your goals, intentions, and wellness? What are the challenges you are facing? What else comes up during your day to reflect on?

MY DAILY VIBE

"I always did something i was a little not ready to do. I think that's how you grow. When there's that moment of "wow, i'm really not sure I can do this," and you push through those moments, thats when you have a breakthrough."

— MARISSA MAYER

Date: _____

(MY) WELL-BEING CHECK IN:
How I'm feeling

....
....
....

(MY) GRATITUDE TODAY:
What, who and things I'm grateful for

....
....
....

(MY) INTENTION FOR TODAY:
What I hope/intend to accomplish or even create today?

....
....
....

(MY) GOAL FOR WHAT I'M WORKING ON AND CREATING:

....
....
....

I AM:
My affirmation for today

....

ADDITIONAL NOTES, THOUGHTS, REFLECTIONS, VIBES AND GRATITUDE:

What are you doing to get closer to your goals, intentions, and wellness? What are the challenges you are facing? What else comes up during your day to reflect on?

MY DAILY VIBE

"I began to realize how important it was to be an enthusiast in life. If you are interested in something, no matter what it is, go at it full speed. Embrace it with both arms, hug it, love it and above all become passionate about it. Lukewarm is no good."

- ROALD DAHL

Date: _____

(MY) WELL-BEING CHECK IN:
How I'm feeling

....
....
....

(MY) GRATITUDE TODAY:
What, who and things I'm grateful for

....
....
....

(MY) INTENTION FOR TODAY:
What I hope/intend to accomplish or even create today?

....
....
....

(MY) GOAL FOR WHAT I'M WORKING ON AND CREATING:

....
....
....

I AM:
My affirmation for today

ADDITIONAL NOTES, THOUGHTS, REFLECTIONS, VIBES AND GRATITUDE:

What are you doing to get closer to your goals, intentions, and wellness? What are the challenges you are facing? What else comes up during your day to reflect on?

MY DAILY VIBE

"I can choose to let it define me, confine me, refine me, outshine me, or I can choose to move on and leave it behind me."

- JOHN C. MAXWELL

Date: _____

(MY) WELL-BEING CHECK IN:
How I'm feeling

....
....
....

(MY) GRATITUDE TODAY:
What, who and things I'm grateful for

....
....
....

(MY) INTENTION FOR TODAY:
What I hope/intend to accomplish or even create today?

....
....
....

(MY) GOAL FOR WHAT I'M WORKING ON AND CREATING:

....
....
....

I AM:
My affirmation for today

ADDITIONAL NOTES, THOUGHTS, REFLECTIONS, VIBES AND GRATITUDE:

What are you doing to get closer to your goals, intentions, and wellness? What are the challenges you are facing? What else comes up during your day to reflect on?

MY DAILY VIBE

"I will persist until I succeed."
- OG MANDINO

Date: _____

❤️ (MY) WELL-BEING CHECK IN:
How I'm feeling

....
....
....

🙌 (MY) GRATITUDE TODAY:
What, who and things I'm grateful for

....
....
....

📅 (MY) INTENTION FOR TODAY:
What I hope/intend to accomplish or even create today?

....
....
....

🎯 (MY) GOAL FOR WHAT I'M WORKING ON AND CREATING:

....
....
....

💪 I AM:
My affirmation for today

ADDITIONAL NOTES, THOUGHTS, REFLECTIONS, VIBES AND GRATITUDE:

What are you doing to get closer to your goals, intentions, and wellness? What are the challenges you are facing? What else comes up during your day to reflect on?

MY DAILY VIBE

"I'm not here to be average I'm here to be awesome."

Date: _____

♥ (MY) WELL-BEING CHECK IN:
How I'm feeling

....
....
....

🙌 (MY) GRATITUDE TODAY:
What, who and things I'm grateful for

....
....
....

📅 (MY) INTENTION FOR TODAY:
What I hope/intend to accomplish or even create today?

....
....
....

🎯 (MY) GOAL FOR WHAT I'M WORKING ON AND CREATING:

....
....
....

💪 I AM:
My affirmation for today

ADDITIONAL NOTES, THOUGHTS, REFLECTIONS, VIBES AND GRATITUDE:

What are you doing to get closer to your goals, intentions, and wellness? What are the challenges you are facing? What else comes up during your day to reflect on?

MY DAILY VIBE

"I've failed over and over and over again in my life... That's why I succeed."
— MICHAEL JORDAN

Date: _____

♥ (MY) WELL-BEING CHECK IN:
How I'm feeling

....
....
....

🙌 (MY) GRATITUDE TODAY:
What, who and things I'm grateful for

....
....
....

📅 (MY) INTENTION FOR TODAY:
What I hope/intend to accomplish or even create today?

....
....
....

🎯 (MY) GOAL FOR WHAT I'M WORKING ON AND CREATING:

....
....
....

💪 I AM:
My affirmation for today

ADDITIONAL NOTES, THOUGHTS, REFLECTIONS, VIBES AND GRATITUDE:

What are you doing to get closer to your goals, intentions, and wellness? What are the challenges you are facing? What else comes up during your day to reflect on?

MY DAILY VIBE

"I've learned from experience that part of our happiness or misery depends on our dispositions, not our circumstances."

- MARTHA WASHINGTON

Date: _____

(MY) WELL-BEING CHECK IN:
How I'm feeling

....
....
....

(MY) GRATITUDE TODAY:
What, who and things I'm grateful for

....
....
....

(MY) INTENTION FOR TODAY:
What I hope/intend to accomplish or even create today?

....
....
....

(MY) GOAL FOR WHAT I'M WORKING ON AND CREATING:

....
....
....

I AM:
My affirmation for today

ADDITIONAL NOTES, THOUGHTS, REFLECTIONS, VIBES AND GRATITUDE:

What are you doing to get closer to your goals, intentions, and wellness? What are the challenges you are facing? What else comes up during your day to reflect on?

MY DAILY VIBE

"If another can easily anger you, it is because you are off balance with yourself."

Date: _____

(MY) WELL-BEING CHECK IN:
How I'm feeling

....
....
....

(MY) GRATITUDE TODAY:
What, who and things I'm grateful for

....
....
....

(MY) INTENTION FOR TODAY:
What I hope/intend to accomplish or even create today?

....
....
....

(MY) GOAL FOR WHAT I'M WORKING ON AND CREATING:

....
....
....

I AM:
My affirmation for today

ADDITIONAL NOTES, THOUGHTS, REFLECTIONS, VIBES AND GRATITUDE:

What are you doing to get closer to your goals, intentions, and wellness? What are the challenges you are facing? What else comes up during your day to reflect on?

MY DAILY VIBE

"If anyone hasn't told you today. You're AWESOME"
- IAN D.

Date: _____

(MY) WELL-BEING CHECK IN:
How I'm feeling

....
....
....

(MY) GRATITUDE TODAY:
What, who and things I'm grateful for

....
....
....

(MY) INTENTION FOR TODAY:
What I hope/intend to accomplish or even create today?

....
....
....

(MY) GOAL FOR WHAT I'M WORKING ON AND CREATING:

....
....
....

I AM:
My affirmation for today

ADDITIONAL NOTES, THOUGHTS, REFLECTIONS, VIBES AND GRATITUDE:

What are you doing to get closer to your goals, intentions, and wellness? What are the challenges you are facing? What else comes up during your day to reflect on?

MY DAILY VIBE

"If i quit now, I will soon be back to where I started. And where I started was desperately wishing to be where I am now."

Date: _____

❤️ (MY) WELL-BEING CHECK IN:
How I'm feeling

....
....
....

🙌 (MY) GRATITUDE TODAY:
What, who and things I'm grateful for

....
....
....

📅 (MY) INTENTION FOR TODAY:
What I hope/intend to accomplish or even create today?

....
....
....

🎯 (MY) GOAL FOR WHAT I'M WORKING ON AND CREATING:

....
....
....

💪 I AM:
My affirmation for today

ADDITIONAL NOTES, THOUGHTS, REFLECTIONS, VIBES AND GRATITUDE:

What are you doing to get closer to your goals, intentions, and wellness? What are the challenges you are facing? What else comes up during your day to reflect on?

MY DAILY VIBE

"If it wasn't hard everyone would do it. Its the hard that makes it great."
- ERIN FIKE

Date: _____

(MY) WELL-BEING CHECK IN:
How I'm feeling

....
....
....

(MY) GRATITUDE TODAY:
What, who and things I'm grateful for

....
....
....

(MY) INTENTION FOR TODAY:
What I hope/intend to accomplish or even create today?

....
....
....

(MY) GOAL FOR WHAT I'M WORKING ON AND CREATING:

....
....
....

I AM:
My affirmation for today

ADDITIONAL NOTES, THOUGHTS, REFLECTIONS, VIBES AND GRATITUDE:

What are you doing to get closer to your goals, intentions, and wellness? What are the challenges you are facing? What else comes up during your day to reflect on?

MY DAILY VIBE

"If not now, when?"
- HILLEL THE ELDER

Date: _____

❤️ (MY) WELL-BEING CHECK IN:
How I'm feeling

....
....
....

🙌 (MY) GRATITUDE TODAY:
What, who and things I'm grateful for

....
....
....

📅 (MY) INTENTION FOR TODAY:
What I hope/intend to accomplish or even create today?

....
....
....

🎯 (MY) GOAL FOR WHAT I'M WORKING ON AND CREATING:

....
....
....

💪 I AM:
My affirmation for today

ADDITIONAL NOTES, THOUGHTS, REFLECTIONS, VIBES AND GRATITUDE:

What are you doing to get closer to your goals, intentions, and wellness? What are the challenges you are facing? What else comes up during your day to reflect on?

DO IT WITH PASSION OR NOT AT ALL

- ROSA NOUCHETTE CAREY

MY TARGETS FOR THE MONTH OF: _____

NOTES

MY DAILY VIBE

"If somebody offers you an amazing opportunity but you are not sure you can do it, say yes – then learn how to do it later."

- RICHARD BRANSON

Date: _____

(MY) WELL-BEING CHECK IN:
How I'm feeling

....
....
....

(MY) GRATITUDE TODAY:
What, who and things I'm grateful for

....
....
....

(MY) INTENTION FOR TODAY:
What I hope/intend to accomplish or even create today?

....
....
....

(MY) GOAL FOR WHAT I'M WORKING ON AND CREATING:

....
....
....

I AM:
My affirmation for today

ADDITIONAL NOTES, THOUGHTS, REFLECTIONS, VIBES AND GRATITUDE:

What are you doing to get closer to your goals, intentions, and wellness? What are the challenges you are facing? What else comes up during your day to reflect on?

MY DAILY VIBE

"If there is no struggle, there is no progress."
- FREDERICK DOUGLASS

Date: _____

(MY) WELL-BEING CHECK IN:
How I'm feeling

....
....
....

(MY) GRATITUDE TODAY:
What, who and things I'm grateful for

....
....
....

(MY) INTENTION FOR TODAY:
What I hope/intend to accomplish or even create today?

....
....
....

(MY) GOAL FOR WHAT I'M WORKING ON AND CREATING:

....
....
....

I AM:
My affirmation for today

ADDITIONAL NOTES, THOUGHTS, REFLECTIONS, VIBES AND GRATITUDE:

What are you doing to get closer to your goals, intentions, and wellness? What are the challenges you are facing? What else comes up during your day to reflect on?

MY DAILY VIBE

"If you are persistent, you will get it. If you are consistent you will keep it."
- HARVEY MACKAYS

Date: _____

(MY) WELL-BEING CHECK IN:
How I'm feeling

....
....
....

(MY) GRATITUDE TODAY:
What, who and things I'm grateful for

....
....
....

(MY) INTENTION FOR TODAY:
What I hope/intend to accomplish or even create today?

....
....
....

(MY) GOAL FOR WHAT I'M WORKING ON AND CREATING:

....
....
....

I AM:
My affirmation for today

ADDITIONAL NOTES, THOUGHTS, REFLECTIONS, VIBES AND GRATITUDE:

What are you doing to get closer to your goals, intentions, and wellness? What are the challenges you are facing? What else comes up during your day to reflect on?

MY DAILY VIBE

"If you aren't willing to work hard for it, then you probably don't really want it."

Date: _____

(MY) WELL-BEING CHECK IN:
How I'm feeling

....
....
....

(MY) GRATITUDE TODAY:
What, who and things I'm grateful for

....
....
....

(MY) INTENTION FOR TODAY:
What I hope/intend to accomplish or even create today?

....
....
....

(MY) GOAL FOR WHAT I'M WORKING ON AND CREATING:

....
....
....

I AM:
My affirmation for today

ADDITIONAL NOTES, THOUGHTS, REFLECTIONS, VIBES AND GRATITUDE:

What are you doing to get closer to your goals, intentions, and wellness? What are the challenges you are facing? What else comes up during your day to reflect on?

MY DAILY VIBE

"If you believe in yourself enough and know what you want, you're going to make it happen."

- MARIAH CAREY

Date: _____

(MY) WELL-BEING CHECK IN:
How I'm feeling

....
....
....

(MY) GRATITUDE TODAY:
What, who and things I'm grateful for

....
....
....

(MY) INTENTION FOR TODAY:
What I hope/intend to accomplish or even create today?

....
....
....

(MY) GOAL FOR WHAT I'M WORKING ON AND CREATING:

....
....
....

I AM:
My affirmation for today

ADDITIONAL NOTES, THOUGHTS, REFLECTIONS, VIBES AND GRATITUDE:

What are you doing to get closer to your goals, intentions, and wellness? What are the challenges you are facing? What else comes up during your day to reflect on?

MY DAILY VIBE

"If you can imagine it, you can achieve it; if you can dream it, you can become it."

- WILLIAM ARTHUR WARD

Date: _____

(MY) WELL-BEING CHECK IN:
How I'm feeling

....
....
....

(MY) GRATITUDE TODAY:
What, who and things I'm grateful for

....
....
....

(MY) INTENTION FOR TODAY:
What I hope/intend to accomplish or even create today?

....
....
....

(MY) GOAL FOR WHAT I'M WORKING ON AND CREATING:

....
....
....

I AM:
My affirmation for today

....

ADDITIONAL NOTES, THOUGHTS, REFLECTIONS, VIBES AND GRATITUDE:

What are you doing to get closer to your goals, intentions, and wellness? What are the challenges you are facing? What else comes up during your day to reflect on?

MY DAILY VIBE

"If you can see it in your mind, you can hold it in your hand."

Date: _____

(MY) WELL-BEING CHECK IN:
How I'm feeling

....
....
....

(MY) GRATITUDE TODAY:
What, who and things I'm grateful for

....
....
....

(MY) INTENTION FOR TODAY:
What I hope/intend to accomplish or even create today?

....
....
....

(MY) GOAL FOR WHAT I'M WORKING ON AND CREATING:

....
....
....

I AM:
My affirmation for today

ADDITIONAL NOTES, THOUGHTS, REFLECTIONS, VIBES AND GRATITUDE:

What are you doing to get closer to your goals, intentions, and wellness? What are the challenges you are facing? What else comes up during your day to reflect on?

MY DAILY VIBE

"If you can't fly, run. If you can't Run, Walk. If you can't walk, Crawl. By all means, keep moving"

- DR. MARTIN LUTHER KING JR.

Date: _____

(MY) WELL-BEING CHECK IN:
How I'm feeling

....
....
....

(MY) GRATITUDE TODAY:
What, who and things I'm grateful for

....
....
....

(MY) INTENTION FOR TODAY:
What I hope/intend to accomplish or even create today?

....
....
....

(MY) GOAL FOR WHAT I'M WORKING ON AND CREATING:

....
....
....

I AM:
My affirmation for today

ADDITIONAL NOTES, THOUGHTS, REFLECTIONS, VIBES AND GRATITUDE:

What are you doing to get closer to your goals, intentions, and wellness? What are the challenges you are facing? What else comes up during your day to reflect on?

MY DAILY VIBE

"If you continuously compete with others you become bitter, but if you continuously compete with yourself you become better."

- MARIE BLANCHARD

Date: _____

(MY) WELL-BEING CHECK IN:
How I'm feeling

....
....
....

(MY) GRATITUDE TODAY:
What, who and things I'm grateful for

....
....
....

(MY) INTENTION FOR TODAY:
What I hope/intend to accomplish or even create today?

....
....
....

(MY) GOAL FOR WHAT I'M WORKING ON AND CREATING:

....
....
....

I AM:
My affirmation for today

ADDITIONAL NOTES, THOUGHTS, REFLECTIONS, VIBES AND GRATITUDE:

What are you doing to get closer to your goals, intentions, and wellness? What are the challenges you are facing? What else comes up during your day to reflect on?

MY DAILY VIBE

"If you don't build your own dream, someone else will hire you to help them build theirs."

- TONY A. GASKINS JR.

Date: _____

(MY) WELL-BEING CHECK IN:
How I'm feeling

....
....
....

(MY) GRATITUDE TODAY:
What, who and things I'm grateful for

....
....
....

(MY) INTENTION FOR TODAY:
What I hope/intend to accomplish or even create today?

....
....
....

(MY) GOAL FOR WHAT I'M WORKING ON AND CREATING:

....
....
....

I AM:
My affirmation for today

ADDITIONAL NOTES, THOUGHTS, REFLECTIONS, VIBES AND GRATITUDE:

What are you doing to get closer to your goals, intentions, and wellness? What are the challenges you are facing? What else comes up during your day to reflect on?

MY DAILY VIBE

"If you don't go after what you want, you'll never have it. If you don't ask the answer is always no. If you don't step forward, you are always in the same pleace."

— NORA ROBERTS

Date: _____

(MY) WELL-BEING CHECK IN:
How I'm feeling

....
....
....

(MY) GRATITUDE TODAY:
What, who and things I'm grateful for

....
....
....

(MY) INTENTION FOR TODAY:
What I hope/intend to accomplish or even create today?

....
....
....

(MY) GOAL FOR WHAT I'M WORKING ON AND CREATING:

....
....
....

I AM:
My affirmation for today

ADDITIONAL NOTES, THOUGHTS, REFLECTIONS, VIBES AND GRATITUDE:

What are you doing to get closer to your goals, intentions, and wellness? What are the challenges you are facing? What else comes up during your day to reflect on?

MY DAILY VIBE

"If you don't take risks you will always work for someone who does."

Date: _____

(MY) WELL-BEING CHECK IN:
How I'm feeling

....

....

....

(MY) GRATITUDE TODAY:
What, who and things I'm grateful for

....

....

....

(MY) INTENTION FOR TODAY:
What I hope/intend to accomplish or even create today?

....

....

....

(MY) GOAL FOR WHAT I'M WORKING ON AND CREATING:

....

....

....

I AM:
My affirmation for today

ADDITIONAL NOTES, THOUGHTS, REFLECTIONS, VIBES AND GRATITUDE:

What are you doing to get closer to your goals, intentions, and wellness? What are the challenges you are facing? What else comes up during your day to reflect on?

MY DAILY VIBE

"If you realized how powerful your thoughts are, you would never think a negative thought."

- PEACE PILGRIM

Date: _____

(MY) WELL-BEING CHECK IN:
How I'm feeling

....
....
....

(MY) GRATITUDE TODAY:
What, who and things I'm grateful for

....
....
....

(MY) INTENTION FOR TODAY:
What I hope/intend to accomplish or even create today?

....
....
....

(MY) GOAL FOR WHAT I'M WORKING ON AND CREATING:

....
....
....

I AM:
My affirmation for today

....

ADDITIONAL NOTES, THOUGHTS, REFLECTIONS, VIBES AND GRATITUDE:

What are you doing to get closer to your goals, intentions, and wellness? What are the challenges you are facing? What else comes up during your day to reflect on?

MY DAILY VIBE

"If your actions inspire others to dream more, learn more, do more and become more you are a leader."

— JOHN QUINCY ADAMS

Date: _____

(MY) WELL-BEING CHECK IN:
How I'm feeling

....
....
....

(MY) GRATITUDE TODAY:
What, who and things I'm grateful for

....
....
....

(MY) INTENTION FOR TODAY:
What I hope/intend to accomplish or even create today?

....
....
....

(MY) GOAL FOR WHAT I'M WORKING ON AND CREATING:

....
....
....

I AM:
My affirmation for today

ADDITIONAL NOTES, THOUGHTS, REFLECTIONS, VIBES AND GRATITUDE:

What are you doing to get closer to your goals, intentions, and wellness? What are the challenges you are facing? What else comes up during your day to reflect on?

MY DAILY VIBE

"In a world that's changing so quickly, you're guaranteed to fail if you don't take any risks."

- MARK ZUCKERBERG

Date: _____

(MY) WELL-BEING CHECK IN:
How I'm feeling

....
....
....

(MY) GRATITUDE TODAY:
What, who and things I'm grateful for

....
....
....

(MY) INTENTION FOR TODAY:
What I hope/intend to accomplish or even create today?

....
....
....

(MY) GOAL FOR WHAT I'M WORKING ON AND CREATING:

....
....
....

I AM:
My affirmation for today

ADDITIONAL NOTES, THOUGHTS, REFLECTIONS, VIBES AND GRATITUDE:

What are you doing to get closer to your goals, intentions, and wellness? What are the challenges you are facing? What else comes up during your day to reflect on?

MY DAILY VIBE

"Invite your mind into the present moment and don't let what you can't control take away from today's joy."

Date: _____

(MY) WELL-BEING CHECK IN:
How I'm feeling

....
....
....

(MY) GRATITUDE TODAY:
What, who and things I'm grateful for

....
....
....

(MY) INTENTION FOR TODAY:
What I hope/intend to accomplish or even create today?

....
....
....

(MY) GOAL FOR WHAT I'M WORKING ON AND CREATING:

....
....
....

I AM:
My affirmation for today

ADDITIONAL NOTES, THOUGHTS, REFLECTIONS, VIBES AND GRATITUDE:

What are you doing to get closer to your goals, intentions, and wellness? What are the challenges you are facing? What else comes up during your day to reflect on?

MY DAILY VIBE

*"It is very important to know who you are.
To make decisions.
To show who you are."*

— MALALA YOUSAFZIA

Date: _____

❤️ (MY) WELL-BEING CHECK IN:
How I'm feeling

....
....
....

🙌 (MY) GRATITUDE TODAY:
What, who and things I'm grateful for

....
....
....

📅 (MY) INTENTION FOR TODAY:
What I hope/intend to accomplish or even create today?

....
....
....

🎯 (MY) GOAL FOR WHAT I'M WORKING ON AND CREATING:

....
....
....

💪 I AM:
My affirmation for today

....

ADDITIONAL NOTES, THOUGHTS, REFLECTIONS, VIBES AND GRATITUDE:

What are you doing to get closer to your goals, intentions, and wellness? What are the challenges you are facing? What else comes up during your day to reflect on?

MY DAILY VIBE

"It is very important to know who you are. To make decisions. To show who you are."

- MALALA YOUSAFZAI

Date: _____

(MY) WELL-BEING CHECK IN:
How I'm feeling

....
....
....

(MY) GRATITUDE TODAY:
What, who and things I'm grateful for

....
....
....

(MY) INTENTION FOR TODAY:
What I hope/intend to accomplish or even create today?

....
....
....

(MY) GOAL FOR WHAT I'M WORKING ON AND CREATING:

....
....
....

I AM:
My affirmation for today

ADDITIONAL NOTES, THOUGHTS, REFLECTIONS, VIBES AND GRATITUDE:

What are you doing to get closer to your goals, intentions, and wellness? What are the challenges you are facing? What else comes up during your day to reflect on?

MY DAILY VIBE

"It may seem difficult at first, but everything is difficult at first."
- MIYAMOTO MUSASHI

Date: _____

(MY) WELL-BEING CHECK IN:
How I'm feeling

(MY) GRATITUDE TODAY:
What, who and things I'm grateful for

(MY) INTENTION FOR TODAY:
What I hope/intend to accomplish or even create today?

(MY) GOAL FOR WHAT I'M WORKING ON AND CREATING:

I AM:
My affirmation for today

ADDITIONAL NOTES, THOUGHTS, REFLECTIONS, VIBES AND GRATITUDE:

What are you doing to get closer to your goals, intentions, and wellness? What are the challenges you are facing? What else comes up during your day to reflect on?

MY DAILY VIBE

"It seems to be a law of nature, inflexible and inexorable that those who will not risk cannot win."

- JOHN PAUL JONES

Date: _____

(MY) WELL-BEING CHECK IN:
How I'm feeling

....
....
....

(MY) GRATITUDE TODAY:
What, who and things I'm grateful for

....
....
....

(MY) INTENTION FOR TODAY:
What I hope/intend to accomplish or even create today?

....
....
....

(MY) GOAL FOR WHAT I'M WORKING ON AND CREATING:

....
....
....

I AM:
My affirmation for today

ADDITIONAL NOTES, THOUGHTS, REFLECTIONS, VIBES AND GRATITUDE:

What are you doing to get closer to your goals, intentions, and wellness? What are the challenges you are facing? What else comes up during your day to reflect on?

MY DAILY VIBE

"It's a terrible thing, I think, in life to wait until you're ready. I have this feeling now that actually no one is ever ready to do anything. There is almost no such thing as ready. There is only now."

-HUGH LAURIE

Date: _____

(MY) WELL-BEING CHECK IN:
How I'm feeling

....
....
....

(MY) GRATITUDE TODAY:
What, who and things I'm grateful for

....
....
....

(MY) INTENTION FOR TODAY:
What I hope/intend to accomplish or even create today?

....
....
....

(MY) GOAL FOR WHAT I'M WORKING ON AND CREATING:

....
....
....

I AM:
My affirmation for today

ADDITIONAL NOTES, THOUGHTS, REFLECTIONS, VIBES AND GRATITUDE:

What are you doing to get closer to your goals, intentions, and wellness? What are the challenges you are facing? What else comes up during your day to reflect on?

MY DAILY VIBE

"Keep calm and just go for it."

Date: _____

(MY) WELL-BEING CHECK IN:
How I'm feeling

....
....
....

(MY) GRATITUDE TODAY:
What, who and things I'm grateful for

....
....
....

(MY) INTENTION FOR TODAY:
What I hope/intend to accomplish or even create today?

....
....
....

(MY) GOAL FOR WHAT I'M WORKING ON AND CREATING:

....
....
....

I AM:
My affirmation for today

ADDITIONAL NOTES, THOUGHTS, REFLECTIONS, VIBES AND GRATITUDE:

What are you doing to get closer to your goals, intentions, and wellness? What are the challenges you are facing? What else comes up during your day to reflect on?

MY DAILY VIBE

"Leaders think and talk about the solutions. Followers think and talk about the problems."

- BRIAN TRACY

Date: _____

(MY) WELL-BEING CHECK IN:
How I'm feeling

(MY) GRATITUDE TODAY:
What, who and things I'm grateful for

(MY) INTENTION FOR TODAY:
What I hope/intend to accomplish or even create today?

(MY) GOAL FOR WHAT I'M WORKING ON AND CREATING:

I AM:
My affirmation for today

ADDITIONAL NOTES, THOUGHTS, REFLECTIONS, VIBES AND GRATITUDE:

What are you doing to get closer to your goals, intentions, and wellness? What are the challenges you are facing? What else comes up during your day to reflect on?

MY DAILY VIBE

"Less and less do you need to force things, until finally you arrive at non-action. When nothing is none, nothing is left undone."

- LAO TZU

Date: _____

(MY) WELL-BEING CHECK IN:
How I'm feeling

(MY) GRATITUDE TODAY:
What, who and things I'm grateful for

(MY) INTENTION FOR TODAY:
What I hope/intend to accomplish or even create today?

(MY) GOAL FOR WHAT I'M WORKING ON AND CREATING:

I AM:
My affirmation for today

ADDITIONAL NOTES, THOUGHTS, REFLECTIONS, VIBES AND GRATITUDE:

What are you doing to get closer to your goals, intentions, and wellness? What are the challenges you are facing? What else comes up during your day to reflect on?

MY DAILY VIBE

"Let go of the thoughts that don't make you strong."

Date: _____

(MY) WELL-BEING CHECK IN:
How I'm feeling

....
....
....

(MY) GRATITUDE TODAY:
What, who and things I'm grateful for

....
....
....

(MY) INTENTION FOR TODAY:
What I hope/intend to accomplish or even create today?

....
....
....

(MY) GOAL FOR WHAT I'M WORKING ON AND CREATING:

....
....
....

I AM:
My affirmation for today

ADDITIONAL NOTES, THOUGHTS, REFLECTIONS, VIBES AND GRATITUDE:

What are you doing to get closer to your goals, intentions, and wellness? What are the challenges you are facing? What else comes up during your day to reflect on?

MY DAILY VIBE

"Let the beauty of what you love be what you do."
- RUMI

Date: _____

♥ (MY) WELL-BEING CHECK IN:
How I'm feeling

....
....
....

🙌 (MY) GRATITUDE TODAY:
What, who and things I'm grateful for

....
....
....

📅 (MY) INTENTION FOR TODAY:
What I hope/intend to accomplish or even create today?

....
....
....

🎯 (MY) GOAL FOR WHAT I'M WORKING ON AND CREATING:

....
....
....

💪 I AM:
My affirmation for today

....

ADDITIONAL NOTES, THOUGHTS, REFLECTIONS, VIBES AND GRATITUDE:

What are you doing to get closer to your goals, intentions, and wellness? What are the challenges you are facing? What else comes up during your day to reflect on?

MY DAILY VIBE

"Life is like a roller coaster. It has its up and downs, but its your choice to scream or enjoy the ride."

— CRYSTAL WARNER

Date: _____

(MY) WELL-BEING CHECK IN:
How I'm feeling

....
....
....

(MY) GRATITUDE TODAY:
What, who and things I'm grateful for

....
....
....

(MY) INTENTION FOR TODAY:
What I hope/intend to accomplish or even create today?

....
....
....

(MY) GOAL FOR WHAT I'M WORKING ON AND CREATING:

....
....
....

I AM:
My affirmation for today

ADDITIONAL NOTES, THOUGHTS, REFLECTIONS, VIBES AND GRATITUDE:

What are you doing to get closer to your goals, intentions, and wellness? What are the challenges you are facing? What else comes up during your day to reflect on?

MY DAILY VIBE

"Like attracts like."

Date: _____

(MY) WELL-BEING CHECK IN:
How I'm feeling

....
....
....

(MY) GRATITUDE TODAY:
What, who and things I'm grateful for

....
....
....

(MY) INTENTION FOR TODAY:
What I hope/intend to accomplish or even create today?

....
....
....

(MY) GOAL FOR WHAT I'M WORKING ON AND CREATING:

....
....
....

I AM:
My affirmation for today

ADDITIONAL NOTES, THOUGHTS, REFLECTIONS, VIBES AND GRATITUDE:

What are you doing to get closer to your goals, intentions, and wellness? What are the challenges you are facing? What else comes up during your day to reflect on?

MY DAILY VIBE

"Little progress is better than no progress at all. Success comes in taking many small steps. If you stumble in a small step it rarely matters. Don't gift wrap the garbage. Let little failures go."

- JOHN C. MAXWELL

Date: _____

(MY) WELL-BEING CHECK IN:
How I'm feeling

....

....

....

(MY) GRATITUDE TODAY:
What, who and things I'm grateful for

....

....

....

(MY) INTENTION FOR TODAY:
What I hope/intend to accomplish or even create today?

....

....

....

(MY) GOAL FOR WHAT I'M WORKING ON AND CREATING:

....

....

....

I AM:
My affirmation for today

ADDITIONAL NOTES, THOUGHTS, REFLECTIONS, VIBES AND GRATITUDE:

What are you doing to get closer to your goals, intentions, and wellness? What are the challenges you are facing? What else comes up during your day to reflect on?

MY DAILY VIBE

"Live quietly in the moment and see the beauty of all before you. The future will take care of itself."

- YOGANADA

Date: _____

(MY) WELL-BEING CHECK IN:
How I'm feeling

_____
_____
_____

(MY) GRATITUDE TODAY:
What, who and things I'm grateful for

_____
_____
_____

(MY) INTENTION FOR TODAY:
What I hope/intend to accomplish or even create today?

_____
_____
_____

(MY) GOAL FOR WHAT I'M WORKING ON AND CREATING:

_____
_____
_____

I AM:
My affirmation for today

ADDITIONAL NOTES, THOUGHTS, REFLECTIONS, VIBES AND GRATITUDE:

What are you doing to get closer to your goals, intentions, and wellness? What are the challenges you are facing? What else comes up during your day to reflect on?

ALL THINGS ARE WORKING FOR YOUR GOOD, BE ENCOURAGED! INHALE GRATITUDE, EXHALE JOY AND PEACE. SMILE, BREATHE AND GO SLOWLY.

- IAN DAVIS

MY TARGETS FOR THE MONTH OF: _____

NOTES

MY DAILY VIBE

*"Live without pretending, Love without depending,
Listen without defending, Speak without offending."*

- DRAKE

Date: _____

(MY) WELL-BEING CHECK IN:
How I'm feeling

....
....
....

(MY) GRATITUDE TODAY:
What, who and things I'm grateful for

....
....
....

(MY) INTENTION FOR TODAY:
What I hope/intend to accomplish or even create today?

....
....
....

(MY) GOAL FOR WHAT I'M WORKING ON AND CREATING:

....
....
....

I AM:
My affirmation for today

ADDITIONAL NOTES, THOUGHTS, REFLECTIONS, VIBES AND GRATITUDE:

What are you doing to get closer to your goals, intentions, and wellness? What are the challenges you are facing? What else comes up during your day to reflect on?

MY DAILY VIBE

"Living Mindfully is not about forcing positivity all the time. It is instead seeing the picture as a whole, acknowledging it, and remembering to keep an open mind towards all aspects of it."

— NICOLE ADDISON

Date: _____

(MY) WELL-BEING CHECK IN:
How I'm feeling

(MY) GRATITUDE TODAY:
What, who and things I'm grateful for

(MY) INTENTION FOR TODAY:
What I hope/intend to accomplish or even create today?

(MY) GOAL FOR WHAT I'M WORKING ON AND CREATING:

I AM:
My affirmation for today

ADDITIONAL NOTES, THOUGHTS, REFLECTIONS, VIBES AND GRATITUDE:

What are you doing to get closer to your goals, intentions, and wellness? What are the challenges you are facing? What else comes up during your day to reflect on?

MY DAILY VIBE

"Look for something positive in each day, even if some days you have to look a little harder."

Date: _____

(MY) WELL-BEING CHECK IN:
How I'm feeling

....
....
....

(MY) GRATITUDE TODAY:
What, who and things I'm grateful for

....
....
....

(MY) INTENTION FOR TODAY:
What I hope/intend to accomplish or even create today?

....
....
....

(MY) GOAL FOR WHAT I'M WORKING ON AND CREATING:

....
....
....

I AM:
My affirmation for today

ADDITIONAL NOTES, THOUGHTS, REFLECTIONS, VIBES AND GRATITUDE:

What are you doing to get closer to your goals, intentions, and wellness? What are the challenges you are facing? What else comes up during your day to reflect on?

MY DAILY VIBE

"Look well into thyself; there is a source of strength which will always spring up if thou wilt always look."

- MARCUS AURELIUS

Date: _____

(MY) WELL-BEING CHECK IN:
How I'm feeling

....
....
....

(MY) GRATITUDE TODAY:
What, who and things I'm grateful for

....
....
....

(MY) INTENTION FOR TODAY:
What I hope/intend to accomplish or even create today?

....
....
....

(MY) GOAL FOR WHAT I'M WORKING ON AND CREATING:

....
....
....

I AM:
My affirmation for today

ADDITIONAL NOTES, THOUGHTS, REFLECTIONS, VIBES AND GRATITUDE:

What are you doing to get closer to your goals, intentions, and wellness? What are the challenges you are facing? What else comes up during your day to reflect on?

MY DAILY VIBE

"Love develops our talents and sets us free to use our gifts for special work that we're capable of. The presence of love attracts good. May you be guided to Let your work be an Expression of your love. May you allow love to work in your life as a power for good."

- IAN DAVIS

Date: _____

(MY) WELL-BEING CHECK IN:
How I'm feeling

....
....
....

(MY) GRATITUDE TODAY:
What, who and things I'm grateful for

....
....
....

(MY) INTENTION FOR TODAY:
What I hope/intend to accomplish or even create today?

....
....
....

(MY) GOAL FOR WHAT I'M WORKING ON AND CREATING:

....
....
....

I AM:
My affirmation for today

ADDITIONAL NOTES, THOUGHTS, REFLECTIONS, VIBES AND GRATITUDE:

What are you doing to get closer to your goals, intentions, and wellness? What are the challenges you are facing? What else comes up during your day to reflect on?

MY DAILY VIBE

"Love governs all. Creation springs from love And the essence of creativeness is Love of life. Such love guides us To do something better, bigger or More enlightening than done before. The perfect seed of love is within."

- FRANK ZAPPA

Date: _____

(MY) WELL-BEING CHECK IN:
How I'm feeling

....
....
....

(MY) GRATITUDE TODAY:
What, who and things I'm grateful for

....
....
....

(MY) INTENTION FOR TODAY:
What I hope/intend to accomplish or even create today?

....
....
....

(MY) GOAL FOR WHAT I'M WORKING ON AND CREATING:

....
....
....

I AM:
My affirmation for today

ADDITIONAL NOTES, THOUGHTS, REFLECTIONS, VIBES AND GRATITUDE:

What are you doing to get closer to your goals, intentions, and wellness? What are the challenges you are facing? What else comes up during your day to reflect on?

MY DAILY VIBE

"Love is life and we are love. Love creates, Love produces, Love heals, Love comforts, Love guides and illuminates. There is no limit to love in the universe and all of it is available to you."

- IAN DAVIS

Date: _____

(MY) WELL-BEING CHECK IN:
How I'm feeling

....
....
....

(MY) GRATITUDE TODAY:
What, who and things I'm grateful for

....
....
....

(MY) INTENTION FOR TODAY:
What I hope/intend to accomplish or even create today?

....
....
....

(MY) GOAL FOR WHAT I'M WORKING ON AND CREATING:

....
....
....

I AM:
My affirmation for today

ADDITIONAL NOTES, THOUGHTS, REFLECTIONS, VIBES AND GRATITUDE:

What are you doing to get closer to your goals, intentions, and wellness? What are the challenges you are facing? What else comes up during your day to reflect on?

MY DAILY VIBE

"Love never fails. With love, we're free from worry, Judgement and fear. With love, all work is easy. May you create, work, perform your tasks, and serve with love. May you work with love to add all things to humanity and to yourself. May you love others as you love yourself."

- IAN DAVIS

Date: _____

❤️ (MY) WELL-BEING CHECK IN:
How I'm feeling

....
....
....

🙌 (MY) GRATITUDE TODAY:
What, who and things I'm grateful for

....
....
....

📅 (MY) INTENTION FOR TODAY:
What I hope/intend to accomplish or even create today?

....
....
....

🎯 (MY) GOAL FOR WHAT I'M WORKING ON AND CREATING:

....
....
....

💪 I AM:
My affirmation for today

ADDITIONAL NOTES, THOUGHTS, REFLECTIONS, VIBES AND GRATITUDE:

What are you doing to get closer to your goals, intentions, and wellness? What are the challenges you are facing? What else comes up during your day to reflect on?

MY DAILY VIBE

"Make it happen."

Date: _____

♥ (MY) WELL-BEING CHECK IN:
How I'm feeling

....
....
....

👐 (MY) GRATITUDE TODAY:
What, who and things I'm grateful for

....
....
....

📅 (MY) INTENTION FOR TODAY:
What I hope/intend to accomplish or even create today?

....
....
....

🎯 (MY) GOAL FOR WHAT I'M WORKING ON AND CREATING:

....
....
....

💪 I AM:
My affirmation for today

ADDITIONAL NOTES, THOUGHTS, REFLECTIONS, VIBES AND GRATITUDE:

What are you doing to get closer to your goals, intentions, and wellness? What are the challenges you are facing? What else comes up during your day to reflect on?

MY DAILY VIBE

"Make no small plans."
- NICCOLO MACHIAVELI

Date: _____

❤️ (MY) WELL-BEING CHECK IN:
How I'm feeling

....
....
....

🙌 (MY) GRATITUDE TODAY:
What, who and things I'm grateful for

....
....
....

📅 (MY) INTENTION FOR TODAY:
What I hope/intend to accomplish or even create today?

....
....
....

🎯 (MY) GOAL FOR WHAT I'M WORKING ON AND CREATING:

....
....
....

💪 I AM:
My affirmation for today

ADDITIONAL NOTES, THOUGHTS, REFLECTIONS, VIBES AND GRATITUDE:

What are you doing to get closer to your goals, intentions, and wellness? What are the challenges you are facing? What else comes up during your day to reflect on?

MY DAILY VIBE

"Make sure you visualize what you really want, not what someone else wants for you."

- JERRY GILLIES

Date: _____

(MY) WELL-BEING CHECK IN:
How I'm feeling

....
....
....

(MY) GRATITUDE TODAY:
What, who and things I'm grateful for

....
....
....

(MY) INTENTION FOR TODAY:
What I hope/intend to accomplish or even create today?

....
....
....

(MY) GOAL FOR WHAT I'M WORKING ON AND CREATING:

....
....
....

I AM:
My affirmation for today

....

ADDITIONAL NOTES, THOUGHTS, REFLECTIONS, VIBES AND GRATITUDE:

What are you doing to get closer to your goals, intentions, and wellness? What are the challenges you are facing? What else comes up during your day to reflect on?

MY DAILY VIBE

"Make your dreams happen."

Date: _____

❤️ (MY) WELL-BEING CHECK IN:
How I'm feeling

....
....
....

🙌 (MY) GRATITUDE TODAY:
What, who and things I'm grateful for

....
....
....

📅 (MY) INTENTION FOR TODAY:
What I hope/intend to accomplish or even create today?

....
....
....

🎯 (MY) GOAL FOR WHAT I'M WORKING ON AND CREATING:

....
....
....

💪 I AM:
My affirmation for today

....

ADDITIONAL NOTES, THOUGHTS, REFLECTIONS, VIBES AND GRATITUDE:

What are you doing to get closer to your goals, intentions, and wellness? What are the challenges you are facing? What else comes up during your day to reflect on?

MY DAILY VIBE

"May you adjust your minds habits, your approach to situations, your mood, your inner nature, your self-talk and your overall outlook on life. May you use thinking that's nourishing, supportive and healing for your well-being. Inhale growth, exhale and release, a smile."

- IAN DAVIS

Date: _____

(MY) WELL-BEING CHECK IN:
How I'm feeling

....
....
....

(MY) GRATITUDE TODAY:
What, who and things I'm grateful for

....
....
....

(MY) INTENTION FOR TODAY:
What I hope/intend to accomplish or even create today?

....
....
....

(MY) GOAL FOR WHAT I'M WORKING ON AND CREATING:

....
....
....

I AM:
My affirmation for today

ADDITIONAL NOTES, THOUGHTS, REFLECTIONS, VIBES AND GRATITUDE:

What are you doing to get closer to your goals, intentions, and wellness? What are the challenges you are facing? What else comes up during your day to reflect on?

MY DAILY VIBE

"MAY YOU BE HELD IN AND WITH LOVE, ALWAYS. MAY YOU BE FREE FROM ANY SUFFERING. MAY IT BE SO."

— IAN DAVIS

Date: _____

(MY) WELL-BEING CHECK IN:
How I'm feeling

....
....
....

(MY) GRATITUDE TODAY:
What, who and things I'm grateful for

....
....
....

(MY) INTENTION FOR TODAY:
What I hope/intend to accomplish or even create today?

....
....
....

(MY) GOAL FOR WHAT I'M WORKING ON AND CREATING:

....
....
....

I AM:
My affirmation for today

ADDITIONAL NOTES, THOUGHTS, REFLECTIONS, VIBES AND GRATITUDE:

What are you doing to get closer to your goals, intentions, and wellness? What are the challenges you are facing? What else comes up during your day to reflect on?

MY DAILY VIBE

"May you be mindful, present in each moment and aware noticing any feelings and sensations that come up. May you go within to help yourself. Inhale, present moment, exhale, wonderful moment."

- IAN DAVIS

Date: _____

(MY) WELL-BEING CHECK IN:
How I'm feeling

....

....

....

(MY) GRATITUDE TODAY:
What, who and things I'm grateful for

....

....

....

(MY) INTENTION FOR TODAY:
What I hope/intend to accomplish or even create today?

....

....

....

(MY) GOAL FOR WHAT I'M WORKING ON AND CREATING:

....

....

....

I AM:
My affirmation for today

ADDITIONAL NOTES, THOUGHTS, REFLECTIONS, VIBES AND GRATITUDE:

What are you doing to get closer to your goals, intentions, and wellness? What are the challenges you are facing? What else comes up during your day to reflect on?

MY DAILY VIBE

"May you be mindful, with a present Moment awareness and continue To help yourself. Choose what you give your attention and power to and how you respond. Deep inhale, exhale and release: awareness."

— IAN DAVIS

Date: _____

♡ (MY) WELL-BEING CHECK IN:
How I'm feeling

....

....

....

🙌 (MY) GRATITUDE TODAY:
What, who and things I'm grateful for

....

....

....

📅 (MY) INTENTION FOR TODAY:
What I hope/intend to accomplish or even create today?

....

....

....

🎯 (MY) GOAL FOR WHAT I'M WORKING ON AND CREATING:

....

....

....

💪 I AM:
My affirmation for today

ADDITIONAL NOTES, THOUGHTS, REFLECTIONS, VIBES AND GRATITUDE:

What are you doing to get closer to your goals, intentions, and wellness? What are the challenges you are facing? What else comes up during your day to reflect on?

MY DAILY VIBE

"MAY YOU HAVE AN AMAZING AND ABUNDANT WEEK. MAY YOU CULTIVATE GOOD THOUGHTS AND ALWAYS REMAIN POSITIVE AND OPTIMISTIC. MAY YOU HAVE PEACE OF MIND, MAY YOU BE YOUR BEST AND HIGHEST SELF."

— IAN DAVIS

Date: _____

(MY) WELL-BEING CHECK IN:
How I'm feeling

....
....
....

(MY) GRATITUDE TODAY:
What, who and things I'm grateful for

....
....
....

(MY) INTENTION FOR TODAY:
What I hope/intend to accomplish or even create today?

....
....
....

(MY) GOAL FOR WHAT I'M WORKING ON AND CREATING:

....
....
....

I AM:
My affirmation for today

....

ADDITIONAL NOTES, THOUGHTS, REFLECTIONS, VIBES AND GRATITUDE:

What are you doing to get closer to your goals, intentions, and wellness? What are the challenges you are facing? What else comes up during your day to reflect on?

MY DAILY VIBE

"MAY YOU HAVE AND EXPERIENCE PEACE ACCEPTING THINGS AS THEY ARE. MAY YOU BE MINDFUL, PRESENT, GO WITHIN AND CONTINUE TO HELP YOURSELF. DEEP INHALE, EXHALE AND RELEASE. MAY IT BE SO."

- IAN DAVIS

Date: _____

(MY) WELL-BEING CHECK IN:
How I'm feeling

....
....
....

(MY) GRATITUDE TODAY:
What, who and things I'm grateful for

....
....
....

(MY) INTENTION FOR TODAY:
What I hope/intend to accomplish or even create today?

....
....
....

(MY) GOAL FOR WHAT I'M WORKING ON AND CREATING:

....
....
....

I AM:
My affirmation for today

ADDITIONAL NOTES, THOUGHTS, REFLECTIONS, VIBES AND GRATITUDE:

What are you doing to get closer to your goals, intentions, and wellness? What are the challenges you are facing? What else comes up during your day to reflect on?

MY DAILY VIBE

"MAY YOU HAVE HEALTH, MAY YOU EXPERIENCE JOY, MAY YOU HAVE PEACE OF MIND, MAY YOU ABOUND IN LOVE. MAY YOU BE MINDFUL, PRESENT, GO WITHIN AND CONTINUE TO HELP YOURSELF."

— IAN DAVIS

Date: _____

(MY) WELL-BEING CHECK IN:
How I'm feeling

(MY) GRATITUDE TODAY:
What, who and things I'm grateful for

(MY) INTENTION FOR TODAY:
What I hope/intend to accomplish or even create today?

(MY) GOAL FOR WHAT I'M WORKING ON AND CREATING:

I AM:
My affirmation for today

ADDITIONAL NOTES, THOUGHTS, REFLECTIONS, VIBES AND GRATITUDE:

What are you doing to get closer to your goals, intentions, and wellness? What are the challenges you are facing? What else comes up during your day to reflect on?

MY DAILY VIBE

"MAY YOU HAVE MENTAL HAPPINESS. MAY YOU HAVE PHYSICAL HAPPINESS. MAY YOU HAVE EASE OF WELL-BEING. MAY IT BE SO."

- IAN DAVIS

Date: _____

(MY) WELL-BEING CHECK IN:
How I'm feeling

....
....
....

(MY) GRATITUDE TODAY:
What, who and things I'm grateful for

....
....
....

(MY) INTENTION FOR TODAY:
What I hope/intend to accomplish or even create today?

....
....
....

(MY) GOAL FOR WHAT I'M WORKING ON AND CREATING:

....
....
....

I AM:
My affirmation for today

ADDITIONAL NOTES, THOUGHTS, REFLECTIONS, VIBES AND GRATITUDE:

What are you doing to get closer to your goals, intentions, and wellness? What are the challenges you are facing? What else comes up during your day to reflect on?

MY DAILY VIBE

"MAY YOU REALIZE YOUR WHOLENESS. MAY YOU HAVE AND EXPERIENCE JOY. MAY YOU USE YOUR SUPPLY OF PEACE, LOVE AND JOY TO MOVE WITH GRACE, POISE AND EASE. MAY YOU BE MINDFUL, PRESENT, GO WITHIN AND CONTINUE TO HELP YOURSELF. MAY IT BE SO."

— IAN DAVIS

Date: _____

(MY) WELL-BEING CHECK IN:
How I'm feeling

(MY) GRATITUDE TODAY:
What, who and things I'm grateful for

(MY) INTENTION FOR TODAY:
What I hope/intend to accomplish or even create today?

(MY) GOAL FOR WHAT I'M WORKING ON AND CREATING:

I AM:
My affirmation for today

ADDITIONAL NOTES, THOUGHTS, REFLECTIONS, VIBES AND GRATITUDE:

What are you doing to get closer to your goals, intentions, and wellness? What are the challenges you are facing? What else comes up during your day to reflect on?

MY DAILY VIBE

"May you recognize there is more good in you than there is bad. You are not the thinker of your thoughts, but the awareness of them. May you banish all fear And function in your power and higher potential more consistently."

— IAN DAVIS

Date: _____

(MY) WELL-BEING CHECK IN:
How I'm feeling

....
....
....

(MY) GRATITUDE TODAY:
What, who and things I'm grateful for

....
....
....

(MY) INTENTION FOR TODAY:
What I hope/intend to accomplish or even create today?

....
....
....

(MY) GOAL FOR WHAT I'M WORKING ON AND CREATING:

....
....
....

I AM:
My affirmation for today

ADDITIONAL NOTES, THOUGHTS, REFLECTIONS, VIBES AND GRATITUDE:

What are you doing to get closer to your goals, intentions, and wellness? What are the challenges you are facing? What else comes up during your day to reflect on?

MY DAILY VIBE

"Mind over Matter."
- SIR CHARLES LYELL

Date: _____

(MY) WELL-BEING CHECK IN:
How I'm feeling

(MY) GRATITUDE TODAY:
What, who and things I'm grateful for

(MY) INTENTION FOR TODAY:
What I hope/intend to accomplish or even create today?

(MY) GOAL FOR WHAT I'M WORKING ON AND CREATING:

I AM:
My affirmation for today

ADDITIONAL NOTES, THOUGHTS, REFLECTIONS, VIBES AND GRATITUDE:

What are you doing to get closer to your goals, intentions, and wellness? What are the challenges you are facing? What else comes up during your day to reflect on?

MY DAILY VIBE

"Never allow waiting to become a habit. Live your dreams and take risks. Life is happening now."

- PAULO COELHO

Date: _____

(MY) WELL-BEING CHECK IN:
How I'm feeling

....
....
....

(MY) GRATITUDE TODAY:
What, who and things I'm grateful for

....
....
....

(MY) INTENTION FOR TODAY:
What I hope/intend to accomplish or even create today?

....
....
....

(MY) GOAL FOR WHAT I'M WORKING ON AND CREATING:

....
....
....

I AM:
My affirmation for today

ADDITIONAL NOTES, THOUGHTS, REFLECTIONS, VIBES AND GRATITUDE:

What are you doing to get closer to your goals, intentions, and wellness? What are the challenges you are facing? What else comes up during your day to reflect on?

MY DAILY VIBE

"Never define your success by somebody else's success. I never looked at another man's grass to tell how green mine should be."

- XZIBIT

Date: _____

(MY) WELL-BEING CHECK IN:
How I'm feeling

....
....
....

(MY) GRATITUDE TODAY:
What, who and things I'm grateful for

....
....
....

(MY) INTENTION FOR TODAY:
What I hope/intend to accomplish or even create today?

....
....
....

(MY) GOAL FOR WHAT I'M WORKING ON AND CREATING:

....
....
....

I AM:
My affirmation for today

ADDITIONAL NOTES, THOUGHTS, REFLECTIONS, VIBES AND GRATITUDE:

What are you doing to get closer to your goals, intentions, and wellness? What are the challenges you are facing? What else comes up during your day to reflect on?

MY DAILY VIBE

"Never make permanent decisions based on temporary feelings."

Date: _____

(MY) WELL-BEING CHECK IN:
How I'm feeling

....
....
....

(MY) GRATITUDE TODAY:
What, who and things I'm grateful for

....
....
....

(MY) INTENTION FOR TODAY:
What I hope/intend to accomplish or even create today?

....
....
....

(MY) GOAL FOR WHAT I'M WORKING ON AND CREATING:

....
....
....

I AM:
My affirmation for today

ADDITIONAL NOTES, THOUGHTS, REFLECTIONS, VIBES AND GRATITUDE:

What are you doing to get closer to your goals, intentions, and wellness? What are the challenges you are facing? What else comes up during your day to reflect on?

MY DAILY VIBE

"Never speak from a place of hate, jealousy, anger or insecurity. Evaluate your words before you let them leave your lips. Sometimes it's best to be quiet."

- TONY A GASKINS JR.

Date: _____

(MY) WELL-BEING CHECK IN:
How I'm feeling

....
....
....

(MY) GRATITUDE TODAY:
What, who and things I'm grateful for

....
....
....

(MY) INTENTION FOR TODAY:
What I hope/intend to accomplish or even create today?

....
....
....

(MY) GOAL FOR WHAT I'M WORKING ON AND CREATING:

....
....
....

I AM:
My affirmation for today

ADDITIONAL NOTES, THOUGHTS, REFLECTIONS, VIBES AND GRATITUDE:

What are you doing to get closer to your goals, intentions, and wellness? What are the challenges you are facing? What else comes up during your day to reflect on?

MY DAILY VIBE

"No person has the right to rain on your dreams."
- DR. MARTIN LUTHER KING JR.

Date: _____

(MY) WELL-BEING CHECK IN:
How I'm feeling

....

....

....

(MY) GRATITUDE TODAY:
What, who and things I'm grateful for

....

....

....

(MY) INTENTION FOR TODAY:
What I hope/intend to accomplish or even create today?

....

....

....

(MY) GOAL FOR WHAT I'M WORKING ON AND CREATING:

....

....

....

I AM:
My affirmation for today

ADDITIONAL NOTES, THOUGHTS, REFLECTIONS, VIBES AND GRATITUDE:

What are you doing to get closer to your goals, intentions, and wellness? What are the challenges you are facing? What else comes up during your day to reflect on?

MY DAILY VIBE

"Nobody is impressed with how good your excuses are."

Date: _____

(MY) WELL-BEING CHECK IN:
How I'm feeling

....
....
....

(MY) GRATITUDE TODAY:
What, who and things I'm grateful for

....
....
....

(MY) INTENTION FOR TODAY:
What I hope/intend to accomplish or even create today?

....
....
....

(MY) GOAL FOR WHAT I'M WORKING ON AND CREATING:

....
....
....

I AM:
My affirmation for today

ADDITIONAL NOTES, THOUGHTS, REFLECTIONS, VIBES AND GRATITUDE:

What are you doing to get closer to your goals, intentions, and wellness? What are the challenges you are facing? What else comes up during your day to reflect on?

DON'T JUDGE EACH DAY BY THE HARVEST YOU REAP BUT BY THE SEEDS THAT YOU PLANT

- ROBERT LOUIS STEVENSON

MY TARGETS FOR THE MONTH OF: _____

NOTES

MY DAILY VIBE

"Nobody is superior nobody is inferior, people are simply unique. Incomparable. you are you. I am I. I have to contribute my potential to life, you have to contribute your potential to life. I have to discover my own being, you have to discover your own being."

- OSHO

Date: _____

(MY) WELL-BEING CHECK IN:
How I'm feeling

....
....
....

(MY) GRATITUDE TODAY:
What, who and things I'm grateful for

....
....
....

(MY) INTENTION FOR TODAY:
What I hope/intend to accomplish or even create today?

....
....
....

(MY) GOAL FOR WHAT I'M WORKING ON AND CREATING:

....
....
....

I AM:
My affirmation for today

ADDITIONAL NOTES, THOUGHTS, REFLECTIONS, VIBES AND GRATITUDE:

What are you doing to get closer to your goals, intentions, and wellness? What are the challenges you are facing? What else comes up during your day to reflect on?

MY DAILY VIBE

"Not every person is going to understand and that's okay/ They have a right to their opinion and you have every right to ignore it."

- JOEL OSTEEN

Date: _____

(MY) WELL-BEING CHECK IN:
How I'm feeling

....
....
....

(MY) GRATITUDE TODAY:
What, who and things I'm grateful for

....
....
....

(MY) INTENTION FOR TODAY:
What I hope/intend to accomplish or even create today?

....
....
....

(MY) GOAL FOR WHAT I'M WORKING ON AND CREATING:

....
....
....

I AM:
My affirmation for today

ADDITIONAL NOTES, THOUGHTS, REFLECTIONS, VIBES AND GRATITUDE:

What are you doing to get closer to your goals, intentions, and wellness? What are the challenges you are facing? What else comes up during your day to reflect on?

MY DAILY VIBE

"Note to self: You can't control how other people receive your energy. Anything you say or do gets filtered through the lens of whatever personal stuff they are going through at the moment. Which is not about you. Just keep doing your thing with as much integrity as possible."

- NANEA HOFFMAN

Date: _____

(MY) WELL-BEING CHECK IN:
How I'm feeling

(MY) GRATITUDE TODAY:
What, who and things I'm grateful for

(MY) INTENTION FOR TODAY:
What I hope/intend to accomplish or even create today?

(MY) GOAL FOR WHAT I'M WORKING ON AND CREATING:

I AM:
My affirmation for today

ADDITIONAL NOTES, THOUGHTS, REFLECTIONS, VIBES AND GRATITUDE:

What are you doing to get closer to your goals, intentions, and wellness? What are the challenges you are facing? What else comes up during your day to reflect on?

MY DAILY VIBE

"Nothing comes ahead of its time, and nothing that ever happened that didn't need to happen."

- BYRON KATIE

Date: _____

(MY) WELL-BEING CHECK IN:
How I'm feeling

....
....
....

(MY) GRATITUDE TODAY:
What, who and things I'm grateful for

....
....
....

(MY) INTENTION FOR TODAY:
What I hope/intend to accomplish or even create today?

....
....
....

(MY) GOAL FOR WHAT I'M WORKING ON AND CREATING:

....
....
....

I AM:
My affirmation for today

ADDITIONAL NOTES, THOUGHTS, REFLECTIONS, VIBES AND GRATITUDE:

What are you doing to get closer to your goals, intentions, and wellness? What are the challenges you are facing? What else comes up during your day to reflect on?

MY DAILY VIBE

"Old ways won't open new doors."

Date: _____

(MY) WELL-BEING CHECK IN:
How I'm feeling

....
....
....

(MY) GRATITUDE TODAY:
What, who and things I'm grateful for

....
....
....

(MY) INTENTION FOR TODAY:
What I hope/intend to accomplish or even create today?

....
....
....

(MY) GOAL FOR WHAT I'M WORKING ON AND CREATING:

....
....
....

I AM:
My affirmation for today

....

ADDITIONAL NOTES, THOUGHTS, REFLECTIONS, VIBES AND GRATITUDE:

What are you doing to get closer to your goals, intentions, and wellness? What are the challenges you are facing? What else comes up during your day to reflect on?

MY DAILY VIBE

"Once you make a decision, the universe starts to conspire to make it happen."

Date: _____

❤️ (MY) WELL-BEING CHECK IN:
How I'm feeling

....
....
....

🙌 (MY) GRATITUDE TODAY:
What, who and things I'm grateful for

....
....
....

📅 (MY) INTENTION FOR TODAY:
What I hope/intend to accomplish or even create today?

....
....
....

🎯 (MY) GOAL FOR WHAT I'M WORKING ON AND CREATING:

....
....
....

💪 I AM:
My affirmation for today

ADDITIONAL NOTES, THOUGHTS, REFLECTIONS, VIBES AND GRATITUDE:

What are you doing to get closer to your goals, intentions, and wellness? What are the challenges you are facing? What else comes up during your day to reflect on?

MY DAILY VIBE

"Once you realize that the road is the goal and that you are always on the road, not to reach a goal, but to enjoy it's beauty and it's wisdom, life ceases to be a task and becomes natural and simple, in itself an ecstasy."

— NISARGADATTA MAHARAJ

Date: _____

(MY) WELL-BEING CHECK IN:
How I'm feeling

....
....
....

(MY) GRATITUDE TODAY:
What, who and things I'm grateful for

....
....
....

(MY) INTENTION FOR TODAY:
What I hope/intend to accomplish or even create today?

....
....
....

(MY) GOAL FOR WHAT I'M WORKING ON AND CREATING:

....
....
....

I AM:
My affirmation for today

ADDITIONAL NOTES, THOUGHTS, REFLECTIONS, VIBES AND GRATITUDE:

What are you doing to get closer to your goals, intentions, and wellness? What are the challenges you are facing? What else comes up during your day to reflect on?

MY DAILY VIBE

"One day you will wake up and there won't be any more time to do the things you've always wanted. Do it now."

- PAULO COELHO

Date: _____

♥ (MY) WELL-BEING CHECK IN:
How I'm feeling

....
....
....

🙌 (MY) GRATITUDE TODAY:
What, who and things I'm grateful for

....
....
....

📅 (MY) INTENTION FOR TODAY:
What I hope/intend to accomplish or even create today?

....
....
....

🎯 (MY) GOAL FOR WHAT I'M WORKING ON AND CREATING:

....
....
....

💪 I AM:
My affirmation for today

ADDITIONAL NOTES, THOUGHTS, REFLECTIONS, VIBES AND GRATITUDE:

What are you doing to get closer to your goals, intentions, and wellness? What are the challenges you are facing? What else comes up during your day to reflect on?

MY DAILY VIBE

"Opportunity does not knock, it presents itself when you beat down the door."
- KYLE CHANDLER

Date: _____

(MY) WELL-BEING CHECK IN:
How I'm feeling

(MY) GRATITUDE TODAY:
What, who and things I'm grateful for

(MY) INTENTION FOR TODAY:
What I hope/intend to accomplish or even create today?

(MY) GOAL FOR WHAT I'M WORKING ON AND CREATING:

I AM:
My affirmation for today

ADDITIONAL NOTES, THOUGHTS, REFLECTIONS, VIBES AND GRATITUDE:

What are you doing to get closer to your goals, intentions, and wellness? What are the challenges you are facing? What else comes up during your day to reflect on?

MY DAILY VIBE

"Optimism is the faith that leads to acheivement."
- HELEN KELLER

Date: _____

(MY) WELL-BEING CHECK IN:
How I'm feeling

....
....
....

(MY) GRATITUDE TODAY:
What, who and things I'm grateful for

....
....
....

(MY) INTENTION FOR TODAY:
What I hope/intend to accomplish or even create today?

....
....
....

(MY) GOAL FOR WHAT I'M WORKING ON AND CREATING:

....
....
....

I AM:
My affirmation for today

ADDITIONAL NOTES, THOUGHTS, REFLECTIONS, VIBES AND GRATITUDE:

What are you doing to get closer to your goals, intentions, and wellness? What are the challenges you are facing? What else comes up during your day to reflect on?

MY DAILY VIBE

"Our purpose in this life is to help others. And if you can't help them at least don't hurt them."

- DALAI LAMA

Date: _____

(MY) WELL-BEING CHECK IN:
How I'm feeling

(MY) GRATITUDE TODAY:
What, who and things I'm grateful for

(MY) INTENTION FOR TODAY:
What I hope/intend to accomplish or even create today?

(MY) GOAL FOR WHAT I'M WORKING ON AND CREATING:

I AM:
My affirmation for today

ADDITIONAL NOTES, THOUGHTS, REFLECTIONS, VIBES AND GRATITUDE:

What are you doing to get closer to your goals, intentions, and wellness? What are the challenges you are facing? What else comes up during your day to reflect on?

MY DAILY VIBE

"Overthinking leads to negative thoughts."

Date: _____

♡ (MY) WELL-BEING CHECK IN:
How I'm feeling

....
....
....

🙌 (MY) GRATITUDE TODAY:
What, who and things I'm grateful for

....
....
....

📅 (MY) INTENTION FOR TODAY:
What I hope/intend to accomplish or even create today?

....
....
....

🎯 (MY) GOAL FOR WHAT I'M WORKING ON AND CREATING:

....
....
....

💪 I AM:
My affirmation for today

ADDITIONAL NOTES, THOUGHTS, REFLECTIONS, VIBES AND GRATITUDE:

What are you doing to get closer to your goals, intentions, and wellness? What are the challenges you are facing? What else comes up during your day to reflect on?

MY DAILY VIBE

"Pain is temporary. Quitting lasts forever."
- LANCE ARMSTRONG

Date: _____

(MY) WELL-BEING CHECK IN:
How I'm feeling

....
....
....

(MY) GRATITUDE TODAY:
What, who and things I'm grateful for

....
....
....

(MY) INTENTION FOR TODAY:
What I hope/intend to accomplish or even create today?

....
....
....

(MY) GOAL FOR WHAT I'M WORKING ON AND CREATING:

....
....
....

I AM:
My affirmation for today

....

ADDITIONAL NOTES, THOUGHTS, REFLECTIONS, VIBES AND GRATITUDE:

What are you doing to get closer to your goals, intentions, and wellness? What are the challenges you are facing? What else comes up during your day to reflect on?

MY DAILY VIBE

"Perhaps, the most important courage is the courage to endure, to persist, to "hang in there" in the face of doubt, uncertainty and criticism from others."

— BRIAN TRACY

Date: _____

(MY) WELL-BEING CHECK IN:
How I'm feeling

_____
_____
_____

(MY) GRATITUDE TODAY:
What, who and things I'm grateful for

_____
_____
_____

(MY) INTENTION FOR TODAY:
What I hope/intend to accomplish or even create today?

_____
_____
_____

(MY) GOAL FOR WHAT I'M WORKING ON AND CREATING:

_____
_____
_____

I AM:
My affirmation for today

ADDITIONAL NOTES, THOUGHTS, REFLECTIONS, VIBES AND GRATITUDE:

What are you doing to get closer to your goals, intentions, and wellness? What are the challenges you are facing? What else comes up during your day to reflect on?

MY DAILY VIBE

"Perserverance is a great element of success. If you knock long enough and loud enough at the gate, you are sure to wake up somebody."

- HENRY WADSWORTH LONGFELLOOW

Date: _____

(MY) WELL-BEING CHECK IN:
How I'm feeling

....
....
....

(MY) GRATITUDE TODAY:
What, who and things I'm grateful for

....
....
....

(MY) INTENTION FOR TODAY:
What I hope/intend to accomplish or even create today?

....
....
....

(MY) GOAL FOR WHAT I'M WORKING ON AND CREATING:

....
....
....

I AM:
My affirmation for today

ADDITIONAL NOTES, THOUGHTS, REFLECTIONS, VIBES AND GRATITUDE:

What are you doing to get closer to your goals, intentions, and wellness? What are the challenges you are facing? What else comes up during your day to reflect on?

MY DAILY VIBE

*"Positive Mind.
Positive Vibes.
Positive life."*

Date: _____

❤️ (MY) WELL-BEING CHECK IN:
How I'm feeling

....
....
....

🙌 (MY) GRATITUDE TODAY:
What, who and things I'm grateful for

....
....
....

📅 (MY) INTENTION FOR TODAY:
What I hope/intend to accomplish or even create today?

....
....
....

🎯 (MY) GOAL FOR WHAT I'M WORKING ON AND CREATING:

....
....
....

💪 I AM:
My affirmation for today

ADDITIONAL NOTES, THOUGHTS, REFLECTIONS, VIBES AND GRATITUDE:

What are you doing to get closer to your goals, intentions, and wellness? What are the challenges you are facing? What else comes up during your day to reflect on?

MY DAILY VIBE

"Practice leaving things be. Let others be themselves -- who are we to judge? -- and let us concentrate on improving our own minds and our own lives instead."

- GYALWANG DRUKPA

Date: _____

(MY) WELL-BEING CHECK IN:
How I'm feeling

(MY) GRATITUDE TODAY:
What, who and things I'm grateful for

(MY) INTENTION FOR TODAY:
What I hope/intend to accomplish or even create today?

(MY) GOAL FOR WHAT I'M WORKING ON AND CREATING:

I AM:
My affirmation for today

ADDITIONAL NOTES, THOUGHTS, REFLECTIONS, VIBES AND GRATITUDE:

What are you doing to get closer to your goals, intentions, and wellness? What are the challenges you are facing? What else comes up during your day to reflect on?

MY DAILY VIBE

"Prove them wrong."

Date: _____

♡ (MY) WELL-BEING CHECK IN:
How I'm feeling

....
....
....

🙌 (MY) GRATITUDE TODAY:
What, who and things I'm grateful for

....
....
....

📅 (MY) INTENTION FOR TODAY:
What I hope/intend to accomplish or even create today?

....
....
....

🎯 (MY) GOAL FOR WHAT I'M WORKING ON AND CREATING:

....
....
....

💪 I AM:
My affirmation for today

ADDITIONAL NOTES, THOUGHTS, REFLECTIONS, VIBES AND GRATITUDE:

What are you doing to get closer to your goals, intentions, and wellness? What are the challenges you are facing? What else comes up during your day to reflect on?

MY DAILY VIBE

"Push harder than yesterday if you want a different tomorrow."

Date: _____

(MY) WELL-BEING CHECK IN:
How I'm feeling

....
....
....

(MY) GRATITUDE TODAY:
What, who and things I'm grateful for

....
....
....

(MY) INTENTION FOR TODAY:
What I hope/intend to accomplish or even create today?

....
....
....

(MY) GOAL FOR WHAT I'M WORKING ON AND CREATING:

....
....
....

I AM:
My affirmation for today

ADDITIONAL NOTES, THOUGHTS, REFLECTIONS, VIBES AND GRATITUDE:

What are you doing to get closer to your goals, intentions, and wellness? What are the challenges you are facing? What else comes up during your day to reflect on?

MY DAILY VIBE

"Radiate boundless love towards the entire world -- above, below, and across -- unhindered, without ill will, without enmity."

— GUATAMA BUDDHA

Date: _____

(MY) WELL-BEING CHECK IN:
How I'm feeling

....
....
....

(MY) GRATITUDE TODAY:
What, who and things I'm grateful for

....
....
....

(MY) INTENTION FOR TODAY:
What I hope/intend to accomplish or even create today?

....
....
....

(MY) GOAL FOR WHAT I'M WORKING ON AND CREATING:

....
....
....

I AM:
My affirmation for today

ADDITIONAL NOTES, THOUGHTS, REFLECTIONS, VIBES AND GRATITUDE:

What are you doing to get closer to your goals, intentions, and wellness? What are the challenges you are facing? What else comes up during your day to reflect on?

MY DAILY VIBE

"Realize deeply that the present moment is all you ever have."
- ECKHART TOLLE

Date: _____

(MY) WELL-BEING CHECK IN:
How I'm feeling

....
....
....

(MY) GRATITUDE TODAY:
What, who and things I'm grateful for

....
....
....

(MY) INTENTION FOR TODAY:
What I hope/intend to accomplish or even create today?

....
....
....

(MY) GOAL FOR WHAT I'M WORKING ON AND CREATING:

....
....
....

I AM:
My affirmation for today

ADDITIONAL NOTES, THOUGHTS, REFLECTIONS, VIBES AND GRATITUDE:

What are you doing to get closer to your goals, intentions, and wellness? What are the challenges you are facing? What else comes up during your day to reflect on?

MY DAILY VIBE

"Recognize the power of the words "I am" When we place limits on our thinking, we don't expand. May you Know and feel all that you are and all that you've been given. May you feel abundance, fulfillment and wholeness."

— IAN DAVIS

Date: _____

(MY) WELL-BEING CHECK IN:
How I'm feeling

(MY) GRATITUDE TODAY:
What, who and things I'm grateful for

(MY) INTENTION FOR TODAY:
What I hope/intend to accomplish or even create today?

(MY) GOAL FOR WHAT I'M WORKING ON AND CREATING:

I AM:
My affirmation for today

ADDITIONAL NOTES, THOUGHTS, REFLECTIONS, VIBES AND GRATITUDE:

What are you doing to get closer to your goals, intentions, and wellness? What are the challenges you are facing? What else comes up during your day to reflect on?

MY DAILY VIBE

"Reject all negative thoughts, Ideas, circumstances and refuse to add them to yourself. Entertain only positive thoughts of Good, abundance, joy, love, kindness and success. Protect your thoughts and dreams, no matter what."

— IAN DAVIS

Date: _____

(MY) WELL-BEING CHECK IN:
How I'm feeling

....
....
....

(MY) GRATITUDE TODAY:
What, who and things I'm grateful for

....
....
....

(MY) INTENTION FOR TODAY:
What I hope/intend to accomplish or even create today?

....
....
....

(MY) GOAL FOR WHAT I'M WORKING ON AND CREATING:

....
....
....

I AM:
My affirmation for today

ADDITIONAL NOTES, THOUGHTS, REFLECTIONS, VIBES AND GRATITUDE:

What are you doing to get closer to your goals, intentions, and wellness? What are the challenges you are facing? What else comes up during your day to reflect on?

MY DAILY VIBE

"Remember that person that gave up? Neither does anyone else."

Date: _____

❤️ (MY) WELL-BEING CHECK IN:
How I'm feeling

....

....

....

🙌 (MY) GRATITUDE TODAY:
What, who and things I'm grateful for

....

....

....

📅 (MY) INTENTION FOR TODAY:
What I hope/intend to accomplish or even create today?

....

....

....

🎯 (MY) GOAL FOR WHAT I'M WORKING ON AND CREATING:

....

....

....

💪 I AM:
My affirmation for today

ADDITIONAL NOTES, THOUGHTS, REFLECTIONS, VIBES AND GRATITUDE:

What are you doing to get closer to your goals, intentions, and wellness? What are the challenges you are facing? What else comes up during your day to reflect on?

MY DAILY VIBE

"Remember who you are. Trust yourself, Believe in yourself and give power to your capabilities. May you be mindful, present and go within to help yourself. May you be your highest and best self. Smile and inhale, exhale and release."

— IAN DAVIS

Date: _____

(MY) WELL-BEING CHECK IN:
How I'm feeling

....
....
....

(MY) GRATITUDE TODAY:
What, who and things I'm grateful for

....
....
....

(MY) INTENTION FOR TODAY:
What I hope/intend to accomplish or even create today?

....
....
....

(MY) GOAL FOR WHAT I'M WORKING ON AND CREATING:

....
....
....

I AM:
My affirmation for today

ADDITIONAL NOTES, THOUGHTS, REFLECTIONS, VIBES AND GRATITUDE:

What are you doing to get closer to your goals, intentions, and wellness? What are the challenges you are facing? What else comes up during your day to reflect on?

MY DAILY VIBE

"Remind yourself that you can't force "it" to be something. You can't force consistency, loyalty, or even honesty. You can't force someone to keep their word, or to communicate, or to realize that something special is right in front of them."

- REYNA BIDDY

Date: _____

(MY) WELL-BEING CHECK IN:
How I'm feeling

....
....
....

(MY) GRATITUDE TODAY:
What, who and things I'm grateful for

....
....
....

(MY) INTENTION FOR TODAY:
What I hope/intend to accomplish or even create today?

....
....
....

(MY) GOAL FOR WHAT I'M WORKING ON AND CREATING:

....
....
....

I AM:
My affirmation for today

ADDITIONAL NOTES, THOUGHTS, REFLECTIONS, VIBES AND GRATITUDE:

What are you doing to get closer to your goals, intentions, and wellness? What are the challenges you are facing? What else comes up during your day to reflect on?

MY DAILY VIBE

"Risk it; go for it. Life always gives you another chance, another go at it. It's very important to take enormous risks."

- MARY QUANT

Date: _____

(MY) WELL-BEING CHECK IN:
How I'm feeling

....

....

....

(MY) GRATITUDE TODAY:
What, who and things I'm grateful for

....

....

....

(MY) INTENTION FOR TODAY:
What I hope/intend to accomplish or even create today?

....

....

....

(MY) GOAL FOR WHAT I'M WORKING ON AND CREATING:

....

....

....

I AM:
My affirmation for today

ADDITIONAL NOTES, THOUGHTS, REFLECTIONS, VIBES AND GRATITUDE:

What are you doing to get closer to your goals, intentions, and wellness? What are the challenges you are facing? What else comes up during your day to reflect on?

MY DAILY VIBE

"Risk vs Reward is the new ROI"
- REBEKAH GRIPPA

Date: _____

(MY) WELL-BEING CHECK IN:
How I'm feeling

....
....
....

(MY) GRATITUDE TODAY:
What, who and things I'm grateful for

....
....
....

(MY) INTENTION FOR TODAY:
What I hope/intend to accomplish or even create today?

....
....
....

(MY) GOAL FOR WHAT I'M WORKING ON AND CREATING:

....
....
....

I AM:
My affirmation for today

ADDITIONAL NOTES, THOUGHTS, REFLECTIONS, VIBES AND GRATITUDE:

What are you doing to get closer to your goals, intentions, and wellness? What are the challenges you are facing? What else comes up during your day to reflect on?

MY DAILY VIBE

"Rivers know this: there is no hurry. We shall get there some day."
- A.A. MILNE

Date: _____

(MY) WELL-BEING CHECK IN:
How I'm feeling

....
....
....

(MY) GRATITUDE TODAY:
What, who and things I'm grateful for

....
....
....

(MY) INTENTION FOR TODAY:
What I hope/intend to accomplish or even create today?

....
....
....

(MY) GOAL FOR WHAT I'M WORKING ON AND CREATING:

....
....
....

I AM:
My affirmation for today

ADDITIONAL NOTES, THOUGHTS, REFLECTIONS, VIBES AND GRATITUDE:

What are you doing to get closer to your goals, intentions, and wellness? What are the challenges you are facing? What else comes up during your day to reflect on?

MY DAILY VIBE

"Running away from your problems is a race you'll never win."

Date: _____

(MY) WELL-BEING CHECK IN:
How I'm feeling

....
....
....

(MY) GRATITUDE TODAY:
What, who and things I'm grateful for

....
....
....

(MY) INTENTION FOR TODAY:
What I hope/intend to accomplish or even create today?

....
....
....

(MY) GOAL FOR WHAT I'M WORKING ON AND CREATING:

....
....
....

I AM:
My affirmation for today

ADDITIONAL NOTES, THOUGHTS, REFLECTIONS, VIBES AND GRATITUDE:

What are you doing to get closer to your goals, intentions, and wellness? What are the challenges you are facing? What else comes up during your day to reflect on?

DON'T PLACE LIMITS
ON YOUR THINKING.
YOU ARE WHOLE,
YOU ARE INFINITE.
YOU ARE DIVINE.
YOU ARE CAPABALE OF
ANY AND EVERYTHING.
AWARENESS HAS THE POWER TO
HEAL AND TRANSFORM YOUR LIFE.
MAY YOU BE MINDFUL, PRESENT,
GO WITHIN AND CONTINUE
TO HELP YOURSELF.
MAY YOU STAY AWARE. BREATHE IN
DEEPLY AND EXHALE EVENLY.

- IAN DAVIS

MY TARGETS FOR THE MONTH OF: _____

NOTES

MY DAILY VIBE

"Seek respect, not attention. It lasts longer."

Date: _____

(MY) WELL-BEING CHECK IN:
How I'm feeling

....
....
....

(MY) GRATITUDE TODAY:
What, who and things I'm grateful for

....
....
....

(MY) INTENTION FOR TODAY:
What I hope/intend to accomplish or even create today?

....
....
....

(MY) GOAL FOR WHAT I'M WORKING ON AND CREATING:

....
....
....

I AM:
My affirmation for today

ADDITIONAL NOTES, THOUGHTS, REFLECTIONS, VIBES AND GRATITUDE:

What are you doing to get closer to your goals, intentions, and wellness? What are the challenges you are facing? What else comes up during your day to reflect on?

MY DAILY VIBE

"Self confidence is the most attractive quality a person can have. How can anyone see how awesome you are if you can't see it yourself?"

Date: _____

(MY) WELL-BEING CHECK IN:
How I'm feeling

....
....
....

(MY) GRATITUDE TODAY:
What, who and things I'm grateful for

....
....
....

(MY) INTENTION FOR TODAY:
What I hope/intend to accomplish or even create today?

....
....
....

(MY) GOAL FOR WHAT I'M WORKING ON AND CREATING:

....
....
....

I AM:
My affirmation for today

ADDITIONAL NOTES, THOUGHTS, REFLECTIONS, VIBES AND GRATITUDE:

What are you doing to get closer to your goals, intentions, and wellness? What are the challenges you are facing? What else comes up during your day to reflect on?

MY DAILY VIBE

*"Sending you good vibes and energy today!
May the long time sun Shine upon you, all love surround you and the bright light within you guide your way on!"*

— IAN DAVIS

Date: _____

(MY) WELL-BEING CHECK IN:
How I'm feeling

....
....
....

(MY) GRATITUDE TODAY:
What, who and things I'm grateful for

....
....
....

(MY) INTENTION FOR TODAY:
What I hope/intend to accomplish or even create today?

....
....
....

(MY) GOAL FOR WHAT I'M WORKING ON AND CREATING:

....
....
....

I AM:
My affirmation for today

ADDITIONAL NOTES, THOUGHTS, REFLECTIONS, VIBES AND GRATITUDE:

What are you doing to get closer to your goals, intentions, and wellness? What are the challenges you are facing? What else comes up during your day to reflect on?

MY DAILY VIBE

"Ships don't sink because of the water around them; ships sink because of the water that gets in them. Don't let what's happening around you get inside you and weigh you down."

— SANVELLO

Date: _____

(MY) WELL-BEING CHECK IN:
How I'm feeling

_____
_____
_____

(MY) GRATITUDE TODAY:
What, who and things I'm grateful for

_____
_____
_____

(MY) INTENTION FOR TODAY:
What I hope/intend to accomplish or even create today?

_____
_____
_____

(MY) GOAL FOR WHAT I'M WORKING ON AND CREATING:

_____
_____
_____

I AM:
My affirmation for today

ADDITIONAL NOTES, THOUGHTS, REFLECTIONS, VIBES AND GRATITUDE:

What are you doing to get closer to your goals, intentions, and wellness? What are the challenges you are facing? What else comes up during your day to reflect on?

MY DAILY VIBE

"Simplify, simplify, simplify."
- THOREAU

Date: _____

(MY) WELL-BEING CHECK IN:
How I'm feeling

....
....
....

(MY) GRATITUDE TODAY:
What, who and things I'm grateful for

....
....
....

(MY) INTENTION FOR TODAY:
What I hope/intend to accomplish or even create today?

....
....
....

(MY) GOAL FOR WHAT I'M WORKING ON AND CREATING:

....
....
....

I AM:
My affirmation for today

ADDITIONAL NOTES, THOUGHTS, REFLECTIONS, VIBES AND GRATITUDE:

What are you doing to get closer to your goals, intentions, and wellness? What are the challenges you are facing? What else comes up during your day to reflect on?

MY DAILY VIBE

"Simply have confidence. Open the door of your mind to admit the positive, the good the beautiful, the aspiring. Know the magnificence inside, that is yours."

- IAN DAVIS

Date: _____

(MY) WELL-BEING CHECK IN:
How I'm feeling

....
....
....

(MY) GRATITUDE TODAY:
What, who and things I'm grateful for

....
....
....

(MY) INTENTION FOR TODAY:
What I hope/intend to accomplish or even create today?

....
....
....

(MY) GOAL FOR WHAT I'M WORKING ON AND CREATING:

....
....
....

I AM:
My affirmation for today

ADDITIONAL NOTES, THOUGHTS, REFLECTIONS, VIBES AND GRATITUDE:

What are you doing to get closer to your goals, intentions, and wellness? What are the challenges you are facing? What else comes up during your day to reflect on?

MY DAILY VIBE

"Smile and let everyone know that today, you're a lot stronger than you were yesterday."

- DRAKE

Date: _____

(MY) WELL-BEING CHECK IN:
How I'm feeling

(MY) GRATITUDE TODAY:
What, who and things I'm grateful for

(MY) INTENTION FOR TODAY:
What I hope/intend to accomplish or even create today?

(MY) GOAL FOR WHAT I'M WORKING ON AND CREATING:

I AM:
My affirmation for today

ADDITIONAL NOTES, THOUGHTS, REFLECTIONS, VIBES AND GRATITUDE:

What are you doing to get closer to your goals, intentions, and wellness? What are the challenges you are facing? What else comes up during your day to reflect on?

MY DAILY VIBE

"Some people want it to happen, some wish it would happen, others make it happen"

- MICHAEL JORDAN

Date: _____

(MY) WELL-BEING CHECK IN:
How I'm feeling

(MY) GRATITUDE TODAY:
What, who and things I'm grateful for

(MY) INTENTION FOR TODAY:
What I hope/intend to accomplish or even create today?

(MY) GOAL FOR WHAT I'M WORKING ON AND CREATING:

I AM:
My affirmation for today

ADDITIONAL NOTES, THOUGHTS, REFLECTIONS, VIBES AND GRATITUDE:

What are you doing to get closer to your goals, intentions, and wellness? What are the challenges you are facing? What else comes up during your day to reflect on?

MY DAILY VIBE

"Sometimes the best way to be happy is to learn to let go of things you tried hard to hold on to that are no longer good for you."

Date: _____

(MY) WELL-BEING CHECK IN:
How I'm feeling

....
....
....

(MY) GRATITUDE TODAY:
What, who and things I'm grateful for

....
....
....

(MY) INTENTION FOR TODAY:
What I hope/intend to accomplish or even create today?

....
....
....

(MY) GOAL FOR WHAT I'M WORKING ON AND CREATING:

....
....
....

I AM:
My affirmation for today

ADDITIONAL NOTES, THOUGHTS, REFLECTIONS, VIBES AND GRATITUDE:

What are you doing to get closer to your goals, intentions, and wellness? What are the challenges you are facing? What else comes up during your day to reflect on?

MY DAILY VIBE

"Sometimes in life, things get messed up, people over-think, over-analyze, and assume. It's human nature though. We aren't perfect and I'm learning this more and more each day. Everybody's beautiful, everybody's flawed and everybody deserves second chances. I don't care what you did, how bad you did it or anything. Sometimes we just weren't ready to make it right the first time. We're only human, remember that."

Date: _____

(MY) WELL-BEING CHECK IN:
How I'm feeling

....
....
....

(MY) GRATITUDE TODAY:
What, who and things I'm grateful for

....
....
....

(MY) INTENTION FOR TODAY:
What I hope/intend to accomplish or even create today?

....
....
....

(MY) GOAL FOR WHAT I'M WORKING ON AND CREATING:

....
....
....

I AM:
My affirmation for today

ADDITIONAL NOTES, THOUGHTS, REFLECTIONS, VIBES AND GRATITUDE:

What are you doing to get closer to your goals, intentions, and wellness? What are the challenges you are facing? What else comes up during your day to reflect on?

MY DAILY VIBE

"Sometimes when you innovate, you make mistakes. It is best to admit them quickly and get on with improving your other innovations."

- STEVE JOBS

Date: _____

(MY) WELL-BEING CHECK IN:
How I'm feeling

(MY) GRATITUDE TODAY:
What, who and things I'm grateful for

(MY) INTENTION FOR TODAY:
What I hope/intend to accomplish or even create today?

(MY) GOAL FOR WHAT I'M WORKING ON AND CREATING:

I AM:
My affirmation for today

ADDITIONAL NOTES, THOUGHTS, REFLECTIONS, VIBES AND GRATITUDE:

What are you doing to get closer to your goals, intentions, and wellness? What are the challenges you are facing? What else comes up during your day to reflect on?

MY DAILY VIBE

"Sometimes you face difficulties not because you're doing something wrong, but because you're doing something right."

- JOEL OSTEEN

Date: _____

(MY) WELL-BEING CHECK IN:
How I'm feeling

....
....
....

(MY) GRATITUDE TODAY:
What, who and things I'm grateful for

....
....
....

(MY) INTENTION FOR TODAY:
What I hope/intend to accomplish or even create today?

....
....
....

(MY) GOAL FOR WHAT I'M WORKING ON AND CREATING:

....
....
....

I AM:
My affirmation for today

ADDITIONAL NOTES, THOUGHTS, REFLECTIONS, VIBES AND GRATITUDE:

What are you doing to get closer to your goals, intentions, and wellness? What are the challenges you are facing? What else comes up during your day to reflect on?

MY DAILY VIBE

"Sometimes your existence gives hope to one person. Your Smile may be a pearl for someone. Your presence might be the desire of the one who loves you dearly. So value yourself."

Date: _____

(MY) WELL-BEING CHECK IN:
How I'm feeling

....
....
....

(MY) GRATITUDE TODAY:
What, who and things I'm grateful for

....
....
....

(MY) INTENTION FOR TODAY:
What I hope/intend to accomplish or even create today?

....
....
....

(MY) GOAL FOR WHAT I'M WORKING ON AND CREATING:

....
....
....

I AM:
My affirmation for today

ADDITIONAL NOTES, THOUGHTS, REFLECTIONS, VIBES AND GRATITUDE:

What are you doing to get closer to your goals, intentions, and wellness? What are the challenges you are facing? What else comes up during your day to reflect on?

MY DAILY VIBE

"Start each day like it's your birthday!"

Date: _____

(MY) WELL-BEING CHECK IN:
How I'm feeling

....
....
....

(MY) GRATITUDE TODAY:
What, who and things I'm grateful for

....
....
....

(MY) INTENTION FOR TODAY:
What I hope/intend to accomplish or even create today?

....
....
....

(MY) GOAL FOR WHAT I'M WORKING ON AND CREATING:

....
....
....

I AM:
My affirmation for today

ADDITIONAL NOTES, THOUGHTS, REFLECTIONS, VIBES AND GRATITUDE:

What are you doing to get closer to your goals, intentions, and wellness? What are the challenges you are facing? What else comes up during your day to reflect on?

MY DAILY VIBE

"Soon, when all is well, you're going to look back on this period of your life and be so glad that you never gave up."

- BRITTANY BURGUNDER

Date: _____

(MY) WELL-BEING CHECK IN:
How I'm feeling

....
....
....

(MY) GRATITUDE TODAY:
What, who and things I'm grateful for

....
....
....

(MY) INTENTION FOR TODAY:
What I hope/intend to accomplish or even create today?

....
....
....

(MY) GOAL FOR WHAT I'M WORKING ON AND CREATING:

....
....
....

I AM:
My affirmation for today

ADDITIONAL NOTES, THOUGHTS, REFLECTIONS, VIBES AND GRATITUDE:

What are you doing to get closer to your goals, intentions, and wellness? What are the challenges you are facing? What else comes up during your day to reflect on?

MY DAILY VIBE

"Stay humble hustle hard."

Date: _____

(MY) WELL-BEING CHECK IN:
How I'm feeling

....
....
....

(MY) GRATITUDE TODAY:
What, who and things I'm grateful for

....
....
....

(MY) INTENTION FOR TODAY:
What I hope/intend to accomplish or even create today?

....
....
....

(MY) GOAL FOR WHAT I'M WORKING ON AND CREATING:

....
....
....

I AM:
My affirmation for today

....

ADDITIONAL NOTES, THOUGHTS, REFLECTIONS, VIBES AND GRATITUDE:

What are you doing to get closer to your goals, intentions, and wellness? What are the challenges you are facing? What else comes up during your day to reflect on?

MY DAILY VIBE

"Stop beating yourself up. You are a work in progress; which means you get there little at a time, not all at once."

- SANVELLO COMMUNITY.

Date: _____

(MY) WELL-BEING CHECK IN:
How I'm feeling

(MY) GRATITUDE TODAY:
What, who and things I'm grateful for

(MY) INTENTION FOR TODAY:
What I hope/intend to accomplish or even create today?

(MY) GOAL FOR WHAT I'M WORKING ON AND CREATING:

I AM:
My affirmation for today

ADDITIONAL NOTES, THOUGHTS, REFLECTIONS, VIBES AND GRATITUDE:

What are you doing to get closer to your goals, intentions, and wellness? What are the challenges you are facing? What else comes up during your day to reflect on?

MY DAILY VIBE

"Stop being afraid of what could go wrong and start being positive about what could go right."

- ZIG ZIGLAR

Date: _____

(MY) WELL-BEING CHECK IN:
How I'm feeling

(MY) GRATITUDE TODAY:
What, who and things I'm grateful for

(MY) INTENTION FOR TODAY:
What I hope/intend to accomplish or even create today?

(MY) GOAL FOR WHAT I'M WORKING ON AND CREATING:

I AM:
My affirmation for today

ADDITIONAL NOTES, THOUGHTS, REFLECTIONS, VIBES AND GRATITUDE:

What are you doing to get closer to your goals, intentions, and wellness? What are the challenges you are facing? What else comes up during your day to reflect on?

MY DAILY VIBE

"Stop doubting yourself, work hard, and make it happen."

Date: _____

❤️ (MY) WELL-BEING CHECK IN:
How I'm feeling

....
....
....

🙌 (MY) GRATITUDE TODAY:
What, who and things I'm grateful for

....
....
....

📅 (MY) INTENTION FOR TODAY:
What I hope/intend to accomplish or even create today?

....
....
....

🎯 (MY) GOAL FOR WHAT I'M WORKING ON AND CREATING:

....
....
....

💪 I AM:
My affirmation for today

ADDITIONAL NOTES, THOUGHTS, REFLECTIONS, VIBES AND GRATITUDE:

What are you doing to get closer to your goals, intentions, and wellness? What are the challenges you are facing? What else comes up during your day to reflect on?

MY DAILY VIBE

"Stop waiting for Friday, for summer, for someone to fall in love with you, for life. Happiness is achieved when you stop waiting for it and make the most of the moment you are in now."

Date: _____

(MY) WELL-BEING CHECK IN:
How I'm feeling

....
....
....

(MY) GRATITUDE TODAY:
What, who and things I'm grateful for

....
....
....

(MY) INTENTION FOR TODAY:
What I hope/intend to accomplish or even create today?

....
....
....

(MY) GOAL FOR WHAT I'M WORKING ON AND CREATING:

....
....
....

I AM:
My affirmation for today

....

ADDITIONAL NOTES, THOUGHTS, REFLECTIONS, VIBES AND GRATITUDE:

What are you doing to get closer to your goals, intentions, and wellness? What are the challenges you are facing? What else comes up during your day to reflect on?

MY DAILY VIBE

"Success is a state of mind. If you want success, start thinking of yourself as a success"

- JOYCE BROTHERS

Date: _____

(MY) WELL-BEING CHECK IN:
How I'm feeling

_____
_____
_____

(MY) GRATITUDE TODAY:
What, who and things I'm grateful for

_____
_____
_____

(MY) INTENTION FOR TODAY:
What I hope/intend to accomplish or even create today?

_____
_____
_____

(MY) GOAL FOR WHAT I'M WORKING ON AND CREATING:

_____
_____
_____

I AM:
My affirmation for today

ADDITIONAL NOTES, THOUGHTS, REFLECTIONS, VIBES AND GRATITUDE:

What are you doing to get closer to your goals, intentions, and wellness? What are the challenges you are facing? What else comes up during your day to reflect on?

MY DAILY VIBE

*"Success is an iceberg people see.
Underneath the surface, persistence, failure, sacrifice, good habits, hard work, dedication."*

- ZIG ZIGLAR

Date: _____

♡ (MY) WELL-BEING CHECK IN:
How I'm feeling

....
....
....

🙌 (MY) GRATITUDE TODAY:
What, who and things I'm grateful for

....
....
....

📅 (MY) INTENTION FOR TODAY:
What I hope/intend to accomplish or even create today?

....
....
....

🎯 (MY) GOAL FOR WHAT I'M WORKING ON AND CREATING:

....
....
....

💪 I AM:
My affirmation for today

ADDITIONAL NOTES, THOUGHTS, REFLECTIONS, VIBES AND GRATITUDE:

What are you doing to get closer to your goals, intentions, and wellness? What are the challenges you are facing? What else comes up during your day to reflect on?

MY DAILY VIBE

"Success is dependent upon the glands – sweat glands."
- ZIG ZIGLAR

Date: _____

(MY) WELL-BEING CHECK IN:
How I'm feeling

....
....
....

(MY) GRATITUDE TODAY:
What, who and things I'm grateful for

....
....
....

(MY) INTENTION FOR TODAY:
What I hope/intend to accomplish or even create today?

....
....
....

(MY) GOAL FOR WHAT I'M WORKING ON AND CREATING:

....
....
....

I AM:
My affirmation for today

ADDITIONAL NOTES, THOUGHTS, REFLECTIONS, VIBES AND GRATITUDE:

What are you doing to get closer to your goals, intentions, and wellness? What are the challenges you are facing? What else comes up during your day to reflect on?

MY DAILY VIBE

"Success is liking yourself, liking what you do and liking how you do it."
- MAYA ANGELOU

Date: _____

♡ (MY) WELL-BEING CHECK IN:
How I'm feeling

🙌 (MY) GRATITUDE TODAY:
What, who and things I'm grateful for

📅 (MY) INTENTION FOR TODAY:
What I hope/intend to accomplish or even create today?

🎯 (MY) GOAL FOR WHAT I'M WORKING ON AND CREATING:

💪 I AM:
My affirmation for today

ADDITIONAL NOTES, THOUGHTS, REFLECTIONS, VIBES AND GRATITUDE:

What are you doing to get closer to your goals, intentions, and wellness? What are the challenges you are facing? What else comes up during your day to reflect on?

MY DAILY VIBE

"Success seems to be connected with action. Successful people keep moving. They make mistakes, but they don't quit."

– CONRAD HILTON

Date: _____

(MY) WELL-BEING CHECK IN:
How I'm feeling

(MY) GRATITUDE TODAY:
What, who and things I'm grateful for

(MY) INTENTION FOR TODAY:
What I hope/intend to accomplish or even create today?

(MY) GOAL FOR WHAT I'M WORKING ON AND CREATING:

I AM:
My affirmation for today

ADDITIONAL NOTES, THOUGHTS, REFLECTIONS, VIBES AND GRATITUDE:

What are you doing to get closer to your goals, intentions, and wellness? What are the challenges you are facing? What else comes up during your day to reflect on?

MY DAILY VIBE

"Successful people never worry about what others are doing."

Date: _____

♡ (MY) WELL-BEING CHECK IN:
How I'm feeling

....
....
....

🙌 (MY) GRATITUDE TODAY:
What, who and things I'm grateful for

....
....
....

📅 (MY) INTENTION FOR TODAY:
What I hope/intend to accomplish or even create today?

....
....
....

🎯 (MY) GOAL FOR WHAT I'M WORKING ON AND CREATING:

....
....
....

💪 I AM:
My affirmation for today

ADDITIONAL NOTES, THOUGHTS, REFLECTIONS, VIBES AND GRATITUDE:

What are you doing to get closer to your goals, intentions, and wellness? What are the challenges you are facing? What else comes up during your day to reflect on?

MY DAILY VIBE

"Surround yourself with the dreamers and the doers, the believers and thinkers but most of all, surround yourself with those who see the greatness within you, even when you don't see it yourself."

— EDMUND LEE

Date: _____

(MY) WELL-BEING CHECK IN:
How I'm feeling

(MY) GRATITUDE TODAY:
What, who and things I'm grateful for

(MY) INTENTION FOR TODAY:
What I hope/intend to accomplish or even create today?

(MY) GOAL FOR WHAT I'M WORKING ON AND CREATING:

I AM:
My affirmation for today

ADDITIONAL NOTES, THOUGHTS, REFLECTIONS, VIBES AND GRATITUDE:

What are you doing to get closer to your goals, intentions, and wellness? What are the challenges you are facing? What else comes up during your day to reflect on?

MY DAILY VIBE

"Take risks. Ask the dumb questions, Fail if you have to, and then get up and do it again."

- JACQUELINE NOVOGRATZ

Date: _____

(MY) WELL-BEING CHECK IN:
How I'm feeling

....
....
....

(MY) GRATITUDE TODAY:
What, who and things I'm grateful for

....
....
....

(MY) INTENTION FOR TODAY:
What I hope/intend to accomplish or even create today?

....
....
....

(MY) GOAL FOR WHAT I'M WORKING ON AND CREATING:

....
....
....

I AM:
My affirmation for today

ADDITIONAL NOTES, THOUGHTS, REFLECTIONS, VIBES AND GRATITUDE:

What are you doing to get closer to your goals, intentions, and wellness? What are the challenges you are facing? What else comes up during your day to reflect on?

MY DAILY VIBE

"TTalk is cheap, results are priceless."

Date: _____

(MY) WELL-BEING CHECK IN:
How I'm feeling

....
....
....

(MY) GRATITUDE TODAY:
What, who and things I'm grateful for

....
....
....

(MY) INTENTION FOR TODAY:
What I hope/intend to accomplish or even create today?

....
....
....

(MY) GOAL FOR WHAT I'M WORKING ON AND CREATING:

....
....
....

I AM:
My affirmation for today

ADDITIONAL NOTES, THOUGHTS, REFLECTIONS, VIBES AND GRATITUDE:

What are you doing to get closer to your goals, intentions, and wellness? What are the challenges you are facing? What else comes up during your day to reflect on?

MY DAILY VIBE

"Tetris taught me that when you try to fit in, you'll disappear."

Date: _____

(MY) WELL-BEING CHECK IN:
How I'm feeling

....
....
....

(MY) GRATITUDE TODAY:
What, who and things I'm grateful for

....
....
....

(MY) INTENTION FOR TODAY:
What I hope/intend to accomplish or even create today?

....
....
....

(MY) GOAL FOR WHAT I'M WORKING ON AND CREATING:

....
....
....

I AM:
My affirmation for today

ADDITIONAL NOTES, THOUGHTS, REFLECTIONS, VIBES AND GRATITUDE:

What are you doing to get closer to your goals, intentions, and wellness? What are the challenges you are facing? What else comes up during your day to reflect on?

**EACH OF US HAS A TALENT
AND GIFT GIVEN ESPECIALLY TO US.
THE SEEDS OF SUCCESS AND
HAPPINESS LIE WITHIN EACH OF US.
MAY YOU RECOGNIZE THAT YOU ARE
WHAT YOU CHOOSE TO BE AND KNOW
THAT YOU CHOICE IS MADE IN THE
MIND. ALL THINGS ARE POSSIBLE.**

- IAN DAVIS

MY TARGETS FOR THE MONTH OF: _____

NOTES

MY DAILY VIBE

"The 3 c's in life:
Choice, Chance, Change.
You must make the choice, to take the change if you want anything in life to change."

- FRANK ZAPPA

Date: _____

(MY) WELL-BEING CHECK IN:
How I'm feeling

....
....
....

(MY) GRATITUDE TODAY:
What, who and things I'm grateful for

....
....
....

(MY) INTENTION FOR TODAY:
What I hope/intend to accomplish or even create today?

....
....
....

(MY) GOAL FOR WHAT I'M WORKING ON AND CREATING:

....
....
....

I AM:
My affirmation for today

ADDITIONAL NOTES, THOUGHTS, REFLECTIONS, VIBES AND GRATITUDE:

What are you doing to get closer to your goals, intentions, and wellness? What are the challenges you are facing? What else comes up during your day to reflect on?

MY DAILY VIBE

"The best use of imagination is creativity. The worst use of imagination is anxiety."

— DEEPAK CHOPRA

Date: _____

♡ (MY) WELL-BEING CHECK IN:
How I'm feeling

_____
_____
_____

🙌 (MY) GRATITUDE TODAY:
What, who and things I'm grateful for

_____
_____
_____

📅 (MY) INTENTION FOR TODAY:
What I hope/intend to accomplish or even create today?

_____
_____
_____

🎯 (MY) GOAL FOR WHAT I'M WORKING ON AND CREATING:

_____
_____
_____

💪 I AM:
My affirmation for today

ADDITIONAL NOTES, THOUGHTS, REFLECTIONS, VIBES AND GRATITUDE:

What are you doing to get closer to your goals, intentions, and wellness? What are the challenges you are facing? What else comes up during your day to reflect on?

MY DAILY VIBE

"The biggest communication problem is we do not listen to understand. We listen to reply."

- STEPHEN COVEY

Date: _____

(MY) WELL-BEING CHECK IN:
How I'm feeling

....
....
....

(MY) GRATITUDE TODAY:
What, who and things I'm grateful for

....
....
....

(MY) INTENTION FOR TODAY:
What I hope/intend to accomplish or even create today?

....
....
....

(MY) GOAL FOR WHAT I'M WORKING ON AND CREATING:

....
....
....

I AM:
My affirmation for today

....

ADDITIONAL NOTES, THOUGHTS, REFLECTIONS, VIBES AND GRATITUDE:

What are you doing to get closer to your goals, intentions, and wellness? What are the challenges you are facing? What else comes up during your day to reflect on?

MY DAILY VIBE

"The chambers of thought Within us are precious. We create by our thought and our desire. May you use thinking that's nourishing and Supportive For your well-being. May you have an abundant, fulfilling and great week!"

— IAN DAVIS

Date: _____

(MY) WELL-BEING CHECK IN:
How I'm feeling

(MY) GRATITUDE TODAY:
What, who and things I'm grateful for

(MY) INTENTION FOR TODAY:
What I hope/intend to accomplish or even create today?

(MY) GOAL FOR WHAT I'M WORKING ON AND CREATING:

I AM:
My affirmation for today

ADDITIONAL NOTES, THOUGHTS, REFLECTIONS, VIBES AND GRATITUDE:

What are you doing to get closer to your goals, intentions, and wellness? What are the challenges you are facing? What else comes up during your day to reflect on?

MY DAILY VIBE

"The dictionary is the only place where success comes before work."
- VINCE LOMBARDI

Date: _____

(MY) WELL-BEING CHECK IN:
How I'm feeling

....
....
....

(MY) GRATITUDE TODAY:
What, who and things I'm grateful for

....
....
....

(MY) INTENTION FOR TODAY:
What I hope/intend to accomplish or even create today?

....
....
....

(MY) GOAL FOR WHAT I'M WORKING ON AND CREATING:

....
....
....

I AM:
My affirmation for today

ADDITIONAL NOTES, THOUGHTS, REFLECTIONS, VIBES AND GRATITUDE:

What are you doing to get closer to your goals, intentions, and wellness? What are the challenges you are facing? What else comes up during your day to reflect on?

MY DAILY VIBE

"The dream is free the hustle is sold separately."

Date: _____

♥ (MY) WELL-BEING CHECK IN:
How I'm feeling

....
....
....

🙌 (MY) GRATITUDE TODAY:
What, who and things I'm grateful for

....
....
....

📅 (MY) INTENTION FOR TODAY:
What I hope/intend to accomplish or even create today?

....
....
....

🎯 (MY) GOAL FOR WHAT I'M WORKING ON AND CREATING:

....
....
....

💪 I AM:
My affirmation for today

ADDITIONAL NOTES, THOUGHTS, REFLECTIONS, VIBES AND GRATITUDE:

What are you doing to get closer to your goals, intentions, and wellness? What are the challenges you are facing? What else comes up during your day to reflect on?

MY DAILY VIBE

"The essence of all art is to have pleasure in giving pleasure."
- DALE CARNEGIE

Date: _____

(MY) WELL-BEING CHECK IN:
How I'm feeling

....
....
....

(MY) GRATITUDE TODAY:
What, who and things I'm grateful for

....
....
....

(MY) INTENTION FOR TODAY:
What I hope/intend to accomplish or even create today?

....
....
....

(MY) GOAL FOR WHAT I'M WORKING ON AND CREATING:

....
....
....

I AM:
My affirmation for today

ADDITIONAL NOTES, THOUGHTS, REFLECTIONS, VIBES AND GRATITUDE:

What are you doing to get closer to your goals, intentions, and wellness? What are the challenges you are facing? What else comes up during your day to reflect on?

MY DAILY VIBE

"The Greatest pleasure in life is doing what people say you cannot do."
- WALTER BAGEHOT

Date: _____

(MY) WELL-BEING CHECK IN:
How I'm feeling

....
....
....

(MY) GRATITUDE TODAY:
What, who and things I'm grateful for

....
....
....

(MY) INTENTION FOR TODAY:
What I hope/intend to accomplish or even create today?

....
....
....

(MY) GOAL FOR WHAT I'M WORKING ON AND CREATING:

....
....
....

I AM:
My affirmation for today

ADDITIONAL NOTES, THOUGHTS, REFLECTIONS, VIBES AND GRATITUDE:

What are you doing to get closer to your goals, intentions, and wellness? What are the challenges you are facing? What else comes up during your day to reflect on?

MY DAILY VIBE

"The greatest prison people live in is the fear of what other people think."
- DAVID ICKE

Date: _____

❤️ (MY) WELL-BEING CHECK IN:
How I'm feeling

....
....
....

🙌 (MY) GRATITUDE TODAY:
What, who and things I'm grateful for

....
....
....

📅 (MY) INTENTION FOR TODAY:
What I hope/intend to accomplish or even create today?

....
....
....

🎯 (MY) GOAL FOR WHAT I'M WORKING ON AND CREATING:

....
....
....

💪 I AM:
My affirmation for today

ADDITIONAL NOTES, THOUGHTS, REFLECTIONS, VIBES AND GRATITUDE:

What are you doing to get closer to your goals, intentions, and wellness? What are the challenges you are facing? What else comes up during your day to reflect on?

MY DAILY VIBE

"The meaning of life is to find your gift. The purpose of life is to give it away."
- PABLO PICASSO

Date: _____

(MY) WELL-BEING CHECK IN:
How I'm feeling

(MY) GRATITUDE TODAY:
What, who and things I'm grateful for

(MY) INTENTION FOR TODAY:
What I hope/intend to accomplish or even create today?

(MY) GOAL FOR WHAT I'M WORKING ON AND CREATING:

I AM:
My affirmation for today

ADDITIONAL NOTES, THOUGHTS, REFLECTIONS, VIBES AND GRATITUDE:

What are you doing to get closer to your goals, intentions, and wellness? What are the challenges you are facing? What else comes up during your day to reflect on?

MY DAILY VIBE

"The moment you doubt whether you can fly, you cease forever to be able to do it."

- J.M BARRIE

Date: _____

(MY) WELL-BEING CHECK IN:
How I'm feeling

_____
_____
_____

(MY) GRATITUDE TODAY:
What, who and things I'm grateful for

_____
_____
_____

(MY) INTENTION FOR TODAY:
What I hope/intend to accomplish or even create today?

_____
_____
_____

(MY) GOAL FOR WHAT I'M WORKING ON AND CREATING:

_____
_____
_____

I AM:
My affirmation for today

ADDITIONAL NOTES, THOUGHTS, REFLECTIONS, VIBES AND GRATITUDE:

What are you doing to get closer to your goals, intentions, and wellness? What are the challenges you are facing? What else comes up during your day to reflect on?

MY DAILY VIBE

"The more you are motivated by love, the more fearless and free your actions will be."

- DALAI LAMA

Date: _____

(MY) WELL-BEING CHECK IN:
How I'm feeling

(MY) GRATITUDE TODAY:
What, who and things I'm grateful for

(MY) INTENTION FOR TODAY:
What I hope/intend to accomplish or even create today?

(MY) GOAL FOR WHAT I'M WORKING ON AND CREATING:

I AM:
My affirmation for today

ADDITIONAL NOTES, THOUGHTS, REFLECTIONS, VIBES AND GRATITUDE:

What are you doing to get closer to your goals, intentions, and wellness? What are the challenges you are facing? What else comes up during your day to reflect on?

MY DAILY VIBE

"The most important thing is to try and inspire people so that they can be great in whatever they want to do."

— KOBE BRYANT

Date: _____

(MY) WELL-BEING CHECK IN:
How I'm feeling

_____
_____
_____

(MY) GRATITUDE TODAY:
What, who and things I'm grateful for

_____
_____
_____

(MY) INTENTION FOR TODAY:
What I hope/intend to accomplish or even create today?

_____
_____
_____

(MY) GOAL FOR WHAT I'M WORKING ON AND CREATING:

_____
_____
_____

I AM:
My affirmation for today

ADDITIONAL NOTES, THOUGHTS, REFLECTIONS, VIBES AND GRATITUDE:

What are you doing to get closer to your goals, intentions, and wellness? What are the challenges you are facing? What else comes up during your day to reflect on?

MY DAILY VIBE

*"The motivation comes from within.
No one can hand it to you, but no one can take it away either."*

Date: _____

♡ (MY) WELL-BEING CHECK IN:
How I'm feeling

....
....
....

🙌 (MY) GRATITUDE TODAY:
What, who and things I'm grateful for

....
....
....

📅 (MY) INTENTION FOR TODAY:
What I hope/intend to accomplish or even create today?

....
....
....

🎯 (MY) GOAL FOR WHAT I'M WORKING ON AND CREATING:

....
....
....

💪 I AM:
My affirmation for today

ADDITIONAL NOTES, THOUGHTS, REFLECTIONS, VIBES AND GRATITUDE:

What are you doing to get closer to your goals, intentions, and wellness? What are the challenges you are facing? What else comes up during your day to reflect on?

MY DAILY VIBE

"The only person you are destined to become is the person you decide to be."
- RALPH WALDO EMERSON

Date: _____

(MY) WELL-BEING CHECK IN:
How I'm feeling

....
....
....

(MY) GRATITUDE TODAY:
What, who and things I'm grateful for

....
....
....

(MY) INTENTION FOR TODAY:
What I hope/intend to accomplish or even create today?

....
....
....

(MY) GOAL FOR WHAT I'M WORKING ON AND CREATING:

....
....
....

I AM:
My affirmation for today

ADDITIONAL NOTES, THOUGHTS, REFLECTIONS, VIBES AND GRATITUDE:

What are you doing to get closer to your goals, intentions, and wellness? What are the challenges you are facing? What else comes up during your day to reflect on?

MY DAILY VIBE

"The only way to do great work is to love what you do. If you haven't found it yet, keep looking. Don't settle."

- STEVE JOBS

Date: _____

(MY) WELL-BEING CHECK IN:
How I'm feeling

....
....
....

(MY) GRATITUDE TODAY:
What, who and things I'm grateful for

....
....
....

(MY) INTENTION FOR TODAY:
What I hope/intend to accomplish or even create today?

....
....
....

(MY) GOAL FOR WHAT I'M WORKING ON AND CREATING:

....
....
....

I AM:
My affirmation for today

....

ADDITIONAL NOTES, THOUGHTS, REFLECTIONS, VIBES AND GRATITUDE:

What are you doing to get closer to your goals, intentions, and wellness? What are the challenges you are facing? What else comes up during your day to reflect on?

MY DAILY VIBE

"The past is a foreign country so we built a wall."

Date: _____

(MY) WELL-BEING CHECK IN:
How I'm feeling

....
....
....

(MY) GRATITUDE TODAY:
What, who and things I'm grateful for

....
....
....

(MY) INTENTION FOR TODAY:
What I hope/intend to accomplish or even create today?

....
....
....

(MY) GOAL FOR WHAT I'M WORKING ON AND CREATING:

....
....
....

I AM:
My affirmation for today

ADDITIONAL NOTES, THOUGHTS, REFLECTIONS, VIBES AND GRATITUDE:

What are you doing to get closer to your goals, intentions, and wellness? What are the challenges you are facing? What else comes up during your day to reflect on?

MY DAILY VIBE

*"The past is no longer.
The Future has not yet come. So look deeply at life as it is."*
- GYALWANG DRUKPA

Date: _____

(MY) WELL-BEING CHECK IN:
How I'm feeling

....
....
....

(MY) GRATITUDE TODAY:
What, who and things I'm grateful for

....
....
....

(MY) INTENTION FOR TODAY:
What I hope/intend to accomplish or even create today?

....
....
....

(MY) GOAL FOR WHAT I'M WORKING ON AND CREATING:

....
....
....

I AM:
My affirmation for today

ADDITIONAL NOTES, THOUGHTS, REFLECTIONS, VIBES AND GRATITUDE:

What are you doing to get closer to your goals, intentions, and wellness? What are the challenges you are facing? What else comes up during your day to reflect on?

MY DAILY VIBE

"THE POWER OF OF THE SPIRIT THAT IS IN AND FLOWS THROUGH YOU IS UNLIMITED. TAP IN! MAY YOU REALIZE YOUR WHOLENESS. MAY YOU BE MINDFUL, PRESENT, GO WITHIN AND CONTINUE TO HELP YOURSELF. DEEP INHALE, EXHALE AND RELEASE. MAY IT BE SO."

- IAN DAVIS

Date: _____

(MY) WELL-BEING CHECK IN:
How I'm feeling

_____
_____
_____

(MY) GRATITUDE TODAY:
What, who and things I'm grateful for

_____
_____
_____

(MY) INTENTION FOR TODAY:
What I hope/intend to accomplish or even create today?

_____
_____
_____

(MY) GOAL FOR WHAT I'M WORKING ON AND CREATING:

_____
_____
_____

I AM:
My affirmation for today

ADDITIONAL NOTES, THOUGHTS, REFLECTIONS, VIBES AND GRATITUDE:

What are you doing to get closer to your goals, intentions, and wellness? What are the challenges you are facing? What else comes up during your day to reflect on?

MY DAILY VIBE

"The power of positive energy lives in every single breath."

Date: _____

(MY) WELL-BEING CHECK IN:
How I'm feeling

....
....
....

(MY) GRATITUDE TODAY:
What, who and things I'm grateful for

....
....
....

(MY) INTENTION FOR TODAY:
What I hope/intend to accomplish or even create today?

....
....
....

(MY) GOAL FOR WHAT I'M WORKING ON AND CREATING:

....
....
....

I AM:
My affirmation for today

....

ADDITIONAL NOTES, THOUGHTS, REFLECTIONS, VIBES AND GRATITUDE:

What are you doing to get closer to your goals, intentions, and wellness? What are the challenges you are facing? What else comes up during your day to reflect on?

MY DAILY VIBE

"The present moment is extremely powerful"
- IAN DAVIS

Date: _____

(MY) WELL-BEING CHECK IN:
How I'm feeling

(MY) GRATITUDE TODAY:
What, who and things I'm grateful for

(MY) INTENTION FOR TODAY:
What I hope/intend to accomplish or even create today?

(MY) GOAL FOR WHAT I'M WORKING ON AND CREATING:

I AM:
My affirmation for today

ADDITIONAL NOTES, THOUGHTS, REFLECTIONS, VIBES AND GRATITUDE:

What are you doing to get closer to your goals, intentions, and wellness? What are the challenges you are facing? What else comes up during your day to reflect on?

MY DAILY VIBE

"The purpose of all life, after al, is to live it, to taste experience to the utmost, to reach out eagerly and without fear for newer and richer experience."

— ELEANOR ROOSEVELT

Date: _____

(MY) WELL-BEING CHECK IN:
How I'm feeling

....
....
....

(MY) GRATITUDE TODAY:
What, who and things I'm grateful for

....
....
....

(MY) INTENTION FOR TODAY:
What I hope/intend to accomplish or even create today?

....
....
....

(MY) GOAL FOR WHAT I'M WORKING ON AND CREATING:

....
....
....

I AM:
My affirmation for today

....

ADDITIONAL NOTES, THOUGHTS, REFLECTIONS, VIBES AND GRATITUDE:

What are you doing to get closer to your goals, intentions, and wellness? What are the challenges you are facing? What else comes up during your day to reflect on?

MY DAILY VIBE

"The purpose of life is a life of purpose."

Date: _____

(MY) WELL-BEING CHECK IN:
How I'm feeling

....

....

....

(MY) GRATITUDE TODAY:
What, who and things I'm grateful for

....

....

....

(MY) INTENTION FOR TODAY:
What I hope/intend to accomplish or even create today?

....

....

....

(MY) GOAL FOR WHAT I'M WORKING ON AND CREATING:

....

....

....

I AM:
My affirmation for today

ADDITIONAL NOTES, THOUGHTS, REFLECTIONS, VIBES AND GRATITUDE:

What are you doing to get closer to your goals, intentions, and wellness? What are the challenges you are facing? What else comes up during your day to reflect on?

MY DAILY VIBE

"The quality of a person's life is in direct proportion to their commitment to excellent, regardless of their chosen field of endeavor."

- VINCE LOMBARDI

Date: _____

(MY) WELL-BEING CHECK IN:
How I'm feeling

....
....
....

(MY) GRATITUDE TODAY:
What, who and things I'm grateful for

....
....
....

(MY) INTENTION FOR TODAY:
What I hope/intend to accomplish or even create today?

....
....
....

(MY) GOAL FOR WHAT I'M WORKING ON AND CREATING:

....
....
....

I AM:
My affirmation for today

ADDITIONAL NOTES, THOUGHTS, REFLECTIONS, VIBES AND GRATITUDE:

What are you doing to get closer to your goals, intentions, and wellness? What are the challenges you are facing? What else comes up during your day to reflect on?

MY DAILY VIBE

"The secret of success is consistency of purpose."
- BENJAMIN DISRAELI

Date: _____

(MY) WELL-BEING CHECK IN:
How I'm feeling

....
....
....

(MY) GRATITUDE TODAY:
What, who and things I'm grateful for

....
....
....

(MY) INTENTION FOR TODAY:
What I hope/intend to accomplish or even create today?

....
....
....

(MY) GOAL FOR WHAT I'M WORKING ON AND CREATING:

....
....
....

I AM:
My affirmation for today

ADDITIONAL NOTES, THOUGHTS, REFLECTIONS, VIBES AND GRATITUDE:

What are you doing to get closer to your goals, intentions, and wellness? What are the challenges you are facing? What else comes up during your day to reflect on?

MY DAILY VIBE

"The soft overcomes the hard; the gentle overcomes the rigid. Everyone knows this is true, but few can put it into practice."

- LAO TZU

Date: _____

(MY) WELL-BEING CHECK IN:
How I'm feeling

_____
_____
_____

(MY) GRATITUDE TODAY:
What, who and things I'm grateful for

_____
_____
_____

(MY) INTENTION FOR TODAY:
What I hope/intend to accomplish or even create today?

_____
_____
_____

(MY) GOAL FOR WHAT I'M WORKING ON AND CREATING:

_____
_____
_____

I AM:
My affirmation for today

ADDITIONAL NOTES, THOUGHTS, REFLECTIONS, VIBES AND GRATITUDE:

What are you doing to get closer to your goals, intentions, and wellness? What are the challenges you are facing? What else comes up during your day to reflect on?

MY DAILY VIBE

"The struggle you're in today is developing the strength you need for tomorrow."

- ROBERT TEW

Date: _____

(MY) WELL-BEING CHECK IN:
How I'm feeling

(MY) GRATITUDE TODAY:
What, who and things I'm grateful for

(MY) INTENTION FOR TODAY:
What I hope/intend to accomplish or even create today?

(MY) GOAL FOR WHAT I'M WORKING ON AND CREATING:

I AM:
My affirmation for today

ADDITIONAL NOTES, THOUGHTS, REFLECTIONS, VIBES AND GRATITUDE:

What are you doing to get closer to your goals, intentions, and wellness? What are the challenges you are facing? What else comes up during your day to reflect on?

MY DAILY VIBE

"The temptation to quit will be greatest just before you are about to succeed."
-BOB PARSONS

Date: _____

(MY) WELL-BEING CHECK IN:
How I'm feeling

....
....
....

(MY) GRATITUDE TODAY:
What, who and things I'm grateful for

....
....
....

(MY) INTENTION FOR TODAY:
What I hope/intend to accomplish or even create today?

....
....
....

(MY) GOAL FOR WHAT I'M WORKING ON AND CREATING:

....
....
....

I AM:
My affirmation for today

ADDITIONAL NOTES, THOUGHTS, REFLECTIONS, VIBES AND GRATITUDE:

What are you doing to get closer to your goals, intentions, and wellness? What are the challenges you are facing? What else comes up during your day to reflect on?

MY DAILY VIBE

"The things you take for granted someone else is praying for."

Date: _____

(MY) WELL-BEING CHECK IN:
How I'm feeling

....
....
....

(MY) GRATITUDE TODAY:
What, who and things I'm grateful for

....
....
....

(MY) INTENTION FOR TODAY:
What I hope/intend to accomplish or even create today?

....
....
....

(MY) GOAL FOR WHAT I'M WORKING ON AND CREATING:

....
....
....

I AM:
My affirmation for today

ADDITIONAL NOTES, THOUGHTS, REFLECTIONS, VIBES AND GRATITUDE:

What are you doing to get closer to your goals, intentions, and wellness? What are the challenges you are facing? What else comes up during your day to reflect on?

MY DAILY VIBE

"The universe is providing a way for you. Things are aligning. Everything is finally coming together. Get ready to receive. It's all happening for you."

Date: _____

(MY) WELL-BEING CHECK IN:
How I'm feeling

....
....
....

(MY) GRATITUDE TODAY:
What, who and things I'm grateful for

....
....
....

(MY) INTENTION FOR TODAY:
What I hope/intend to accomplish or even create today?

....
....
....

(MY) GOAL FOR WHAT I'M WORKING ON AND CREATING:

....
....
....

I AM:
My affirmation for today

ADDITIONAL NOTES, THOUGHTS, REFLECTIONS, VIBES AND GRATITUDE:

What are you doing to get closer to your goals, intentions, and wellness? What are the challenges you are facing? What else comes up during your day to reflect on?

WITH OUR THOUGHTS, WE MAKE THE WORLD.

– BUDDHA

MY TARGETS FOR THE MONTH OF: _____

NOTES

MY DAILY VIBE

> *"The way you consistently treat, think and talk about others, is your vibration."*
>
> - LALAH DELIA

Date: _____

♡ (MY) WELL-BEING CHECK IN:
How I'm feeling

....

....

....

🙌 (MY) GRATITUDE TODAY:
What, who and things I'm grateful for

....

....

....

📅 (MY) INTENTION FOR TODAY:
What I hope/intend to accomplish or even create today?

....

....

....

🎯 (MY) GOAL FOR WHAT I'M WORKING ON AND CREATING:

....

....

....

💪 I AM:
My affirmation for today

ADDITIONAL NOTES, THOUGHTS, REFLECTIONS, VIBES AND GRATITUDE:

What are you doing to get closer to your goals, intentions, and wellness? What are the challenges you are facing? What else comes up during your day to reflect on?

MY DAILY VIBE

"The way you perceive and react to the world is a choice"
- DAVID FOSTER WALLACE

Date: _____

(MY) WELL-BEING CHECK IN:
How I'm feeling

....
....
....

(MY) GRATITUDE TODAY:
What, who and things I'm grateful for

....
....
....

(MY) INTENTION FOR TODAY:
What I hope/intend to accomplish or even create today?

....
....
....

(MY) GOAL FOR WHAT I'M WORKING ON AND CREATING:

....
....
....

I AM:
My affirmation for today

ADDITIONAL NOTES, THOUGHTS, REFLECTIONS, VIBES AND GRATITUDE:

What are you doing to get closer to your goals, intentions, and wellness? What are the challenges you are facing? What else comes up during your day to reflect on?

MY DAILY VIBE

"There are 7 days in a week and 'Someday' isn't one of them."

Date: _____

(MY) WELL-BEING CHECK IN:
How I'm feeling

....

....

....

(MY) GRATITUDE TODAY:
What, who and things I'm grateful for

....

....

....

(MY) INTENTION FOR TODAY:
What I hope/intend to accomplish or even create today?

....

....

....

(MY) GOAL FOR WHAT I'M WORKING ON AND CREATING:

....

....

....

I AM:
My affirmation for today

ADDITIONAL NOTES, THOUGHTS, REFLECTIONS, VIBES AND GRATITUDE:

What are you doing to get closer to your goals, intentions, and wellness? What are the challenges you are facing? What else comes up during your day to reflect on?

MY DAILY VIBE

"There are only two days in the year that nothing can be done. One is called yesterday and the other is called tomorrow, so today is the right day to love, believe, do and mostly live."

- DALAI LAMA

Date: _____

(MY) WELL-BEING CHECK IN:
How I'm feeling

....
....
....

(MY) GRATITUDE TODAY:
What, who and things I'm grateful for

....
....
....

(MY) INTENTION FOR TODAY:
What I hope/intend to accomplish or even create today?

....
....
....

(MY) GOAL FOR WHAT I'M WORKING ON AND CREATING:

....
....
....

I AM:
My affirmation for today

ADDITIONAL NOTES, THOUGHTS, REFLECTIONS, VIBES AND GRATITUDE:

What are you doing to get closer to your goals, intentions, and wellness? What are the challenges you are facing? What else comes up during your day to reflect on?

MY DAILY VIBE

"There is a great creative power that will work through you. Open your heart and mind to your inner self. May you be mindful, present and continue to help yourself. Deep inhale, exhale and release."

- IAN DAVIS

Date: _____

(MY) WELL-BEING CHECK IN:
How I'm feeling

....
....
....

(MY) GRATITUDE TODAY:
What, who and things I'm grateful for

....
....
....

(MY) INTENTION FOR TODAY:
What I hope/intend to accomplish or even create today?

....
....
....

(MY) GOAL FOR WHAT I'M WORKING ON AND CREATING:

....
....
....

I AM:
My affirmation for today

ADDITIONAL NOTES, THOUGHTS, REFLECTIONS, VIBES AND GRATITUDE:

What are you doing to get closer to your goals, intentions, and wellness? What are the challenges you are facing? What else comes up during your day to reflect on?

MY DAILY VIBE

"There is an ever-present energy of Love within and around you. Allow yourself to receive. May you Connect to the presence of love. May you embody the energy of love."

- IAN DAVIS

Date: _____

♡ (MY) WELL-BEING CHECK IN:
How I'm feeling

....
....
....

🙌 (MY) GRATITUDE TODAY:
What, who and things I'm grateful for

....
....
....

📅 (MY) INTENTION FOR TODAY:
What I hope/intend to accomplish or even create today?

....
....
....

🎯 (MY) GOAL FOR WHAT I'M WORKING ON AND CREATING:

....
....
....

💪 I AM:
My affirmation for today

ADDITIONAL NOTES, THOUGHTS, REFLECTIONS, VIBES AND GRATITUDE:

What are you doing to get closer to your goals, intentions, and wellness? What are the challenges you are facing? What else comes up during your day to reflect on?

MY DAILY VIBE

"There is no passion to be found playing small -- In settling for a life that is less than the one you are capable of living."

- NELSON MANDELA

Date: _____

(MY) WELL-BEING CHECK IN:
How I'm feeling

....
....
....

(MY) GRATITUDE TODAY:
What, who and things I'm grateful for

....
....
....

(MY) INTENTION FOR TODAY:
What I hope/intend to accomplish or even create today?

....
....
....

(MY) GOAL FOR WHAT I'M WORKING ON AND CREATING:

....
....
....

I AM:
My affirmation for today

ADDITIONAL NOTES, THOUGHTS, REFLECTIONS, VIBES AND GRATITUDE:

What are you doing to get closer to your goals, intentions, and wellness? What are the challenges you are facing? What else comes up during your day to reflect on?

MY DAILY VIBE

"There is no such thing as "going back to square one." Even if you feel like you're having to start over, you are trying again with more knowledge, strength & power than you had before. Your journey was never over, it was just waiting for you to find it again."

Date: _____

(MY) WELL-BEING CHECK IN:
How I'm feeling

(MY) GRATITUDE TODAY:
What, who and things I'm grateful for

(MY) INTENTION FOR TODAY:
What I hope/intend to accomplish or even create today?

(MY) GOAL FOR WHAT I'M WORKING ON AND CREATING:

I AM:
My affirmation for today

ADDITIONAL NOTES, THOUGHTS, REFLECTIONS, VIBES AND GRATITUDE:

What are you doing to get closer to your goals, intentions, and wellness? What are the challenges you are facing? What else comes up during your day to reflect on?

MY DAILY VIBE

"There will be haters, doubters, non-believers, and then there will be you proving them wrong."

Date: _____

(MY) WELL-BEING CHECK IN:
How I'm feeling

(MY) GRATITUDE TODAY:
What, who and things I'm grateful for

(MY) INTENTION FOR TODAY:
What I hope/intend to accomplish or even create today?

(MY) GOAL FOR WHAT I'M WORKING ON AND CREATING:

I AM:
My affirmation for today

ADDITIONAL NOTES, THOUGHTS, REFLECTIONS, VIBES AND GRATITUDE:

What are you doing to get closer to your goals, intentions, and wellness? What are the challenges you are facing? What else comes up during your day to reflect on?

MY DAILY VIBE

"Things you are passionate about are not random, they are your calling."
- FABIENNE FREDRICKSON

Date: _____

♡ (MY) WELL-BEING CHECK IN:
How I'm feeling

....
....
....

🙌 (MY) GRATITUDE TODAY:
What, who and things I'm grateful for

....
....
....

📅 (MY) INTENTION FOR TODAY:
What I hope/intend to accomplish or even create today?

....
....
....

🎯 (MY) GOAL FOR WHAT I'M WORKING ON AND CREATING:

....
....
....

💪 I AM:
My affirmation for today

ADDITIONAL NOTES, THOUGHTS, REFLECTIONS, VIBES AND GRATITUDE:

What are you doing to get closer to your goals, intentions, and wellness? What are the challenges you are facing? What else comes up during your day to reflect on?

MY DAILY VIBE

*"Three things you cannot recover in life:
The moment after it's missed, the word after it's said, and the time after it's wasted."*

Date: _____

(MY) WELL-BEING CHECK IN:
How I'm feeling

....
....
....

(MY) GRATITUDE TODAY:
What, who and things I'm grateful for

....
....
....

(MY) INTENTION FOR TODAY:
What I hope/intend to accomplish or even create today?

....
....
....

(MY) GOAL FOR WHAT I'M WORKING ON AND CREATING:

....
....
....

I AM:
My affirmation for today

ADDITIONAL NOTES, THOUGHTS, REFLECTIONS, VIBES AND GRATITUDE:

What are you doing to get closer to your goals, intentions, and wellness? What are the challenges you are facing? What else comes up during your day to reflect on?

MY DAILY VIBE

"Through perserverance many people win success out of what seemed destined to be certain failure"

- BENJAMIN DISRAELI

Date: _____

♥ (MY) WELL-BEING CHECK IN:
How I'm feeling

....
....
....

🙌 (MY) GRATITUDE TODAY:
What, who and things I'm grateful for

....
....
....

📅 (MY) INTENTION FOR TODAY:
What I hope/intend to accomplish or even create today?

....
....
....

🎯 (MY) GOAL FOR WHAT I'M WORKING ON AND CREATING:

....
....
....

💪 I AM:
My affirmation for today

ADDITIONAL NOTES, THOUGHTS, REFLECTIONS, VIBES AND GRATITUDE:

What are you doing to get closer to your goals, intentions, and wellness? What are the challenges you are facing? What else comes up during your day to reflect on?

MY DAILY VIBE

"To all the passionate souls the pioneers the leaders, the wanderers, & the dreamers to the peacemakers and the action takers to the survivors the revolutionaries the healers the lovers the adventurers & the innovators you embody the best of the human spirit. You are what the world needs."

- BENJAMIN DISRAELI

Date: _____

(MY) WELL-BEING CHECK IN:
How I'm feeling

....
....
....

(MY) GRATITUDE TODAY:
What, who and things I'm grateful for

....
....
....

(MY) INTENTION FOR TODAY:
What I hope/intend to accomplish or even create today?

....
....
....

(MY) GOAL FOR WHAT I'M WORKING ON AND CREATING:

....
....
....

I AM:
My affirmation for today

ADDITIONAL NOTES, THOUGHTS, REFLECTIONS, VIBES AND GRATITUDE:

What are you doing to get closer to your goals, intentions, and wellness? What are the challenges you are facing? What else comes up during your day to reflect on?

MY DAILY VIBE

"To have faith is to trust yourself to the water. When you swim you don't grab hold of the water because if you do you will sink and drown. Instead you relax and float."

— ALAN WATTS

Date: _____

♡ (MY) WELL-BEING CHECK IN:
How I'm feeling

....
....
....

🙌 (MY) GRATITUDE TODAY:
What, who and things I'm grateful for

....
....
....

📅 (MY) INTENTION FOR TODAY:
What I hope/intend to accomplish or even create today?

....
....
....

🎯 (MY) GOAL FOR WHAT I'M WORKING ON AND CREATING:

....
....
....

💪 I AM:
My affirmation for today

ADDITIONAL NOTES, THOUGHTS, REFLECTIONS, VIBES AND GRATITUDE:

What are you doing to get closer to your goals, intentions, and wellness? What are the challenges you are facing? What else comes up during your day to reflect on?

MY DAILY VIBE

"To me, success is choice and opportunity."
- HARRISON FORD

Date: _____

♥ (MY) WELL-BEING CHECK IN:
How I'm feeling

....

....

....

👐 (MY) GRATITUDE TODAY:
What, who and things I'm grateful for

....

....

....

📅 (MY) INTENTION FOR TODAY:
What I hope/intend to accomplish or even create today?

....

....

....

🎯 (MY) GOAL FOR WHAT I'M WORKING ON AND CREATING:

....

....

....

💪 I AM:
My affirmation for today

ADDITIONAL NOTES, THOUGHTS, REFLECTIONS, VIBES AND GRATITUDE:

What are you doing to get closer to your goals, intentions, and wellness? What are the challenges you are facing? What else comes up during your day to reflect on?

MY DAILY VIBE

"Today is a gift. May you notice the present that lies Within the present moment. May you succeed and have achievement and prosperity."

— IAN DAVIS

Date: _____

(MY) WELL-BEING CHECK IN:
How I'm feeling

....
....
....

(MY) GRATITUDE TODAY:
What, who and things I'm grateful for

....
....
....

(MY) INTENTION FOR TODAY:
What I hope/intend to accomplish or even create today?

....
....
....

(MY) GOAL FOR WHAT I'M WORKING ON AND CREATING:

....
....
....

I AM:
My affirmation for today

....

ADDITIONAL NOTES, THOUGHTS, REFLECTIONS, VIBES AND GRATITUDE:

What are you doing to get closer to your goals, intentions, and wellness? What are the challenges you are facing? What else comes up during your day to reflect on?

MY DAILY VIBE

"Tough times never last, but tough people do."
- ROBERT H SCHULLER

Date: _____

(MY) WELL-BEING CHECK IN:
How I'm feeling

....
....
....

(MY) GRATITUDE TODAY:
What, who and things I'm grateful for

....
....
....

(MY) INTENTION FOR TODAY:
What I hope/intend to accomplish or even create today?

....
....
....

(MY) GOAL FOR WHAT I'M WORKING ON AND CREATING:

....
....
....

I AM:
My affirmation for today

ADDITIONAL NOTES, THOUGHTS, REFLECTIONS, VIBES AND GRATITUDE:

What are you doing to get closer to your goals, intentions, and wellness? What are the challenges you are facing? What else comes up during your day to reflect on?

MY DAILY VIBE

"TRUST IN YOURSELF. BELIEVE IN YOURSELF. BECOME WHAT YOU BELIEVE. MAY YOU LEARN TO CONTROL YOUR THINKING. MAY YOU THINK POSITIVELY, INSTEAD OF NEGATIVELY. MAY YOU HAVE AN ABUNDANT AND FULFILLING DAY AND WEEK."

— IAN DAVIS

Date: _____

(MY) WELL-BEING CHECK IN:
How I'm feeling

(MY) GRATITUDE TODAY:
What, who and things I'm grateful for

(MY) INTENTION FOR TODAY:
What I hope/intend to accomplish or even create today?

(MY) GOAL FOR WHAT I'M WORKING ON AND CREATING:

I AM:
My affirmation for today

ADDITIONAL NOTES, THOUGHTS, REFLECTIONS, VIBES AND GRATITUDE:

What are you doing to get closer to your goals, intentions, and wellness? What are the challenges you are facing? What else comes up during your day to reflect on?

MY DAILY VIBE

*"Try not. Do, or do not.
There is no try."*

- YODA

Date: _____

(MY) WELL-BEING CHECK IN:
How I'm feeling

....
....
....

(MY) GRATITUDE TODAY:
What, who and things I'm grateful for

....
....
....

(MY) INTENTION FOR TODAY:
What I hope/intend to accomplish or even create today?

....
....
....

(MY) GOAL FOR WHAT I'M WORKING ON AND CREATING:

....
....
....

I AM:
My affirmation for today

ADDITIONAL NOTES, THOUGHTS, REFLECTIONS, VIBES AND GRATITUDE:

What are you doing to get closer to your goals, intentions, and wellness? What are the challenges you are facing? What else comes up during your day to reflect on?

MY DAILY VIBE

"Two things define you. Your patience when you have nothing, and your attitude when you have everything."

Date: _____

(MY) WELL-BEING CHECK IN:
How I'm feeling

....
....
....

(MY) GRATITUDE TODAY:
What, who and things I'm grateful for

....
....
....

(MY) INTENTION FOR TODAY:
What I hope/intend to accomplish or even create today?

....
....
....

(MY) GOAL FOR WHAT I'M WORKING ON AND CREATING:

....
....
....

I AM:
My affirmation for today

ADDITIONAL NOTES, THOUGHTS, REFLECTIONS, VIBES AND GRATITUDE:

What are you doing to get closer to your goals, intentions, and wellness? What are the challenges you are facing? What else comes up during your day to reflect on?

MY DAILY VIBE

"Vision without action is daydream. Action without vision is nightmare."
- JAPANESE PROVERB

Date: _____

(MY) WELL-BEING CHECK IN:
How I'm feeling

(MY) GRATITUDE TODAY:
What, who and things I'm grateful for

(MY) INTENTION FOR TODAY:
What I hope/intend to accomplish or even create today?

(MY) GOAL FOR WHAT I'M WORKING ON AND CREATING:

I AM:
My affirmation for today

ADDITIONAL NOTES, THOUGHTS, REFLECTIONS, VIBES AND GRATITUDE:

What are you doing to get closer to your goals, intentions, and wellness? What are the challenges you are facing? What else comes up during your day to reflect on?

MY DAILY VIBE

"Visualization works if you work hard."

Date: _____

(MY) WELL-BEING CHECK IN:
How I'm feeling

_____
_____
_____

(MY) GRATITUDE TODAY:
What, who and things I'm grateful for

_____
_____
_____

(MY) INTENTION FOR TODAY:
What I hope/intend to accomplish or even create today?

_____
_____
_____

(MY) GOAL FOR WHAT I'M WORKING ON AND CREATING:

_____
_____
_____

I AM:
My affirmation for today

ADDITIONAL NOTES, THOUGHTS, REFLECTIONS, VIBES AND GRATITUDE:

What are you doing to get closer to your goals, intentions, and wellness? What are the challenges you are facing? What else comes up during your day to reflect on?

MY DAILY VIBE

"Visualize clearly, precisely and frequently and it will manifest itself into reality."

Date: _____

(MY) WELL-BEING CHECK IN:
How I'm feeling

....
....
....

(MY) GRATITUDE TODAY:
What, who and things I'm grateful for

....
....
....

(MY) INTENTION FOR TODAY:
What I hope/intend to accomplish or even create today?

....
....
....

(MY) GOAL FOR WHAT I'M WORKING ON AND CREATING:

....
....
....

I AM:
My affirmation for today

ADDITIONAL NOTES, THOUGHTS, REFLECTIONS, VIBES AND GRATITUDE:

What are you doing to get closer to your goals, intentions, and wellness? What are the challenges you are facing? What else comes up during your day to reflect on?

MY DAILY VIBE

*"Wake up.
Kick Ass.
Repeat."*

Date: _____

(MY) WELL-BEING CHECK IN:
How I'm feeling

....
....
....

(MY) GRATITUDE TODAY:
What, who and things I'm grateful for

....
....
....

(MY) INTENTION FOR TODAY:
What I hope/intend to accomplish or even create today?

....
....
....

(MY) GOAL FOR WHAT I'M WORKING ON AND CREATING:

....
....
....

I AM:
My affirmation for today

ADDITIONAL NOTES, THOUGHTS, REFLECTIONS, VIBES AND GRATITUDE:

What are you doing to get closer to your goals, intentions, and wellness? What are the challenges you are facing? What else comes up during your day to reflect on?

MY DAILY VIBE

"Wanting approval from others isn't the problem. The real issue is being too attached to getting approval from others as the only way to feel fulfilled. To put it simply, addiction to approval puts your happiness under the control of others."

Date: _____

(MY) WELL-BEING CHECK IN:
How I'm feeling

....
....
....

(MY) GRATITUDE TODAY:
What, who and things I'm grateful for

....
....
....

(MY) INTENTION FOR TODAY:
What I hope/intend to accomplish or even create today?

....
....
....

(MY) GOAL FOR WHAT I'M WORKING ON AND CREATING:

....
....
....

I AM:
My affirmation for today

ADDITIONAL NOTES, THOUGHTS, REFLECTIONS, VIBES AND GRATITUDE:

What are you doing to get closer to your goals, intentions, and wellness? What are the challenges you are facing? What else comes up during your day to reflect on?

MY DAILY VIBE

"We do not need magic to change the world we carry all the power we need inside ourselves already we have the power to imagine better."

- J.K ROWLING

Date: _____

(MY) WELL-BEING CHECK IN:
How I'm feeling

....
....
....

(MY) GRATITUDE TODAY:
What, who and things I'm grateful for

....
....
....

(MY) INTENTION FOR TODAY:
What I hope/intend to accomplish or even create today?

....
....
....

(MY) GOAL FOR WHAT I'M WORKING ON AND CREATING:

....
....
....

I AM:
My affirmation for today

ADDITIONAL NOTES, THOUGHTS, REFLECTIONS, VIBES AND GRATITUDE:

What are you doing to get closer to your goals, intentions, and wellness? What are the challenges you are facing? What else comes up during your day to reflect on?

MY DAILY VIBE

"We don't appreciate negative vibes around here. Move along."
-DAU

Date: _____

(MY) WELL-BEING CHECK IN:
How I'm feeling

_____
_____
_____

(MY) GRATITUDE TODAY:
What, who and things I'm grateful for

_____
_____
_____

(MY) INTENTION FOR TODAY:
What I hope/intend to accomplish or even create today?

_____
_____
_____

(MY) GOAL FOR WHAT I'M WORKING ON AND CREATING:

_____
_____
_____

I AM:
My affirmation for today

ADDITIONAL NOTES, THOUGHTS, REFLECTIONS, VIBES AND GRATITUDE:

What are you doing to get closer to your goals, intentions, and wellness? What are the challenges you are facing? What else comes up during your day to reflect on?

MY DAILY VIBE

"We learn more by looking for the answer to a question and not finding it than we do from learning the answer itself."

-LLOYD ALEXANDER

Date: _____

(MY) WELL-BEING CHECK IN:
How I'm feeling

(MY) GRATITUDE TODAY:
What, who and things I'm grateful for

(MY) INTENTION FOR TODAY:
What I hope/intend to accomplish or even create today?

(MY) GOAL FOR WHAT I'M WORKING ON AND CREATING:

I AM:
My affirmation for today

ADDITIONAL NOTES, THOUGHTS, REFLECTIONS, VIBES AND GRATITUDE:

What are you doing to get closer to your goals, intentions, and wellness? What are the challenges you are facing? What else comes up during your day to reflect on?

MY DAILY VIBE

"We tend to forget that happiness doesn't come as a result of getting something we don't have, but rather of recognizing and appreciating what we do have."

-FREDERICK KEONIG

Date: _____

(MY) WELL-BEING CHECK IN:
How I'm feeling

....
....
....

(MY) GRATITUDE TODAY:
What, who and things I'm grateful for

....
....
....

(MY) INTENTION FOR TODAY:
What I hope/intend to accomplish or even create today?

....
....
....

(MY) GOAL FOR WHAT I'M WORKING ON AND CREATING:

....
....
....

I AM:
My affirmation for today

ADDITIONAL NOTES, THOUGHTS, REFLECTIONS, VIBES AND GRATITUDE:

What are you doing to get closer to your goals, intentions, and wellness? What are the challenges you are facing? What else comes up during your day to reflect on?

YOUR GIFTS WILL MAKE ROOM FOR YOU. INHALE CONFIDENCE, EXHALE PEACE. IT'S YOURS. TRUST AND BE MINDFUL OF YOUR POWER!

— IAN DAVIS

MY TARGETS FOR THE MONTH OF: _____

NOTES

MY DAILY VIBE

"We're so engaged in doing things to achieve purposes of outer value that we forget that the inner value, the rapture that is associated with being alive, is what it's all about."

— JOSEPH CAMPBELL

Date: _____

(MY) WELL-BEING CHECK IN:
How I'm feeling

_____
_____
_____

(MY) GRATITUDE TODAY:
What, who and things I'm grateful for

_____
_____
_____

(MY) INTENTION FOR TODAY:
What I hope/intend to accomplish or even create today?

_____
_____
_____

(MY) GOAL FOR WHAT I'M WORKING ON AND CREATING:

_____
_____
_____

I AM:
My affirmation for today

ADDITIONAL NOTES, THOUGHTS, REFLECTIONS, VIBES AND GRATITUDE:

What are you doing to get closer to your goals, intentions, and wellness? What are the challenges you are facing? What else comes up during your day to reflect on?

MY DAILY VIBE

"What feels like the end is often the beginning."

Date: _____

(MY) WELL-BEING CHECK IN:
How I'm feeling

....
....
....

(MY) GRATITUDE TODAY:
What, who and things I'm grateful for

....
....
....

(MY) INTENTION FOR TODAY:
What I hope/intend to accomplish or even create today?

....
....
....

(MY) GOAL FOR WHAT I'M WORKING ON AND CREATING:

....
....
....

I AM:
My affirmation for today

ADDITIONAL NOTES, THOUGHTS, REFLECTIONS, VIBES AND GRATITUDE:

What are you doing to get closer to your goals, intentions, and wellness? What are the challenges you are facing? What else comes up during your day to reflect on?

MY DAILY VIBE

"What you've accomplished to date, is tiny in comparison, to the potential within you. May you grow to know the magnificence that is yours. May you allow yourself to receive."

- IAN DAVIS

Date: _____

(MY) WELL-BEING CHECK IN:
How I'm feeling

....
....
....

(MY) GRATITUDE TODAY:
What, who and things I'm grateful for

....
....
....

(MY) INTENTION FOR TODAY:
What I hope/intend to accomplish or even create today?

....
....
....

(MY) GOAL FOR WHAT I'M WORKING ON AND CREATING:

....
....
....

I AM:
My affirmation for today

ADDITIONAL NOTES, THOUGHTS, REFLECTIONS, VIBES AND GRATITUDE:

What are you doing to get closer to your goals, intentions, and wellness? What are the challenges you are facing? What else comes up during your day to reflect on?

MY DAILY VIBE

"Whatever happens, love that."
- MATT KAHN

Date: _____

(MY) WELL-BEING CHECK IN:
How I'm feeling

....
....
....

(MY) GRATITUDE TODAY:
What, who and things I'm grateful for

....
....
....

(MY) INTENTION FOR TODAY:
What I hope/intend to accomplish or even create today?

....
....
....

(MY) GOAL FOR WHAT I'M WORKING ON AND CREATING:

....
....
....

I AM:
My affirmation for today

ADDITIONAL NOTES, THOUGHTS, REFLECTIONS, VIBES AND GRATITUDE:

What are you doing to get closer to your goals, intentions, and wellness? What are the challenges you are facing? What else comes up during your day to reflect on?

MY DAILY VIBE

"Whatever you believe about yourself on the inside is what you will manifest on the outside."

Date: _____

(MY) WELL-BEING CHECK IN:
How I'm feeling

....
....
....

(MY) GRATITUDE TODAY:
What, who and things I'm grateful for

....
....
....

(MY) INTENTION FOR TODAY:
What I hope/intend to accomplish or even create today?

....
....
....

(MY) GOAL FOR WHAT I'M WORKING ON AND CREATING:

....
....
....

I AM:
My affirmation for today

ADDITIONAL NOTES, THOUGHTS, REFLECTIONS, VIBES AND GRATITUDE:

What are you doing to get closer to your goals, intentions, and wellness? What are the challenges you are facing? What else comes up during your day to reflect on?

MY DAILY VIBE

"Whatever you're thinking, think bigger."
- TONY HSIEH

Date: _____

(MY) WELL-BEING CHECK IN:
How I'm feeling

....
....
....

(MY) GRATITUDE TODAY:
What, who and things I'm grateful for

....
....
....

(MY) INTENTION FOR TODAY:
What I hope/intend to accomplish or even create today?

....
....
....

(MY) GOAL FOR WHAT I'M WORKING ON AND CREATING:

....
....
....

I AM:
My affirmation for today

ADDITIONAL NOTES, THOUGHTS, REFLECTIONS, VIBES AND GRATITUDE:

What are you doing to get closer to your goals, intentions, and wellness? What are the challenges you are facing? What else comes up during your day to reflect on?

MY DAILY VIBE

"When I thought I couldn't go I forced myself to keep going. My success is backed on persistence, not luck."

- ESTEE LAUDER

Date: _____

(MY) WELL-BEING CHECK IN:
How I'm feeling

(MY) GRATITUDE TODAY:
What, who and things I'm grateful for

(MY) INTENTION FOR TODAY:
What I hope/intend to accomplish or even create today?

(MY) GOAL FOR WHAT I'M WORKING ON AND CREATING:

I AM:
My affirmation for today

ADDITIONAL NOTES, THOUGHTS, REFLECTIONS, VIBES AND GRATITUDE:

What are you doing to get closer to your goals, intentions, and wellness? What are the challenges you are facing? What else comes up during your day to reflect on?

MY DAILY VIBE

"When something goes wrong in your life, know that its divine, just yell "plot twist" and move on."

Date: _____

(MY) WELL-BEING CHECK IN:
How I'm feeling

....
....
....

(MY) GRATITUDE TODAY:
What, who and things I'm grateful for

....
....
....

(MY) INTENTION FOR TODAY:
What I hope/intend to accomplish or even create today?

....
....
....

(MY) GOAL FOR WHAT I'M WORKING ON AND CREATING:

....
....
....

I AM:
My affirmation for today

ADDITIONAL NOTES, THOUGHTS, REFLECTIONS, VIBES AND GRATITUDE:

What are you doing to get closer to your goals, intentions, and wellness? What are the challenges you are facing? What else comes up during your day to reflect on?

MY DAILY VIBE

"When the mind is at peace, the world too is at peace. Nothing Real, nothing Absent. Not holding on to reality, not getting stuck in the void, you are neither holy nor wise, just an ordinary fellow who has completed his work."

- LAYMAN P'ANG

Date: _____

(MY) WELL-BEING CHECK IN:
How I'm feeling

(MY) GRATITUDE TODAY:
What, who and things I'm grateful for

(MY) INTENTION FOR TODAY:
What I hope/intend to accomplish or even create today?

(MY) GOAL FOR WHAT I'M WORKING ON AND CREATING:

I AM:
My affirmation for today

ADDITIONAL NOTES, THOUGHTS, REFLECTIONS, VIBES AND GRATITUDE:

What are you doing to get closer to your goals, intentions, and wellness? What are the challenges you are facing? What else comes up during your day to reflect on?

MY DAILY VIBE

"When we stop fearing failure, we start being artists."
- ANN VOSKAMP

Date: _____

(MY) WELL-BEING CHECK IN:
How I'm feeling

....
....
....

(MY) GRATITUDE TODAY:
What, who and things I'm grateful for

....
....
....

(MY) INTENTION FOR TODAY:
What I hope/intend to accomplish or even create today?

....
....
....

(MY) GOAL FOR WHAT I'M WORKING ON AND CREATING:

....
....
....

I AM:
My affirmation for today

....

ADDITIONAL NOTES, THOUGHTS, REFLECTIONS, VIBES AND GRATITUDE:

What are you doing to get closer to your goals, intentions, and wellness? What are the challenges you are facing? What else comes up during your day to reflect on?

MY DAILY VIBE

"When you are content to simply be yourself and don't compare or compete, everyone will respect you."

- LAO TZU

Date: _____

(MY) WELL-BEING CHECK IN:
How I'm feeling

(MY) GRATITUDE TODAY:
What, who and things I'm grateful for

(MY) INTENTION FOR TODAY:
What I hope/intend to accomplish or even create today?

(MY) GOAL FOR WHAT I'M WORKING ON AND CREATING:

I AM:
My affirmation for today

ADDITIONAL NOTES, THOUGHTS, REFLECTIONS, VIBES AND GRATITUDE:

What are you doing to get closer to your goals, intentions, and wellness? What are the challenges you are facing? What else comes up during your day to reflect on?

MY DAILY VIBE

"When you become comfortable with uncertainty, infinite possibilities open up in your life."

- ECKHART TOLLE

Date: _____

(MY) WELL-BEING CHECK IN:
How I'm feeling

....
....
....

(MY) GRATITUDE TODAY:
What, who and things I'm grateful for

....
....
....

(MY) INTENTION FOR TODAY:
What I hope/intend to accomplish or even create today?

....
....
....

(MY) GOAL FOR WHAT I'M WORKING ON AND CREATING:

....
....
....

I AM:
My affirmation for today

....

ADDITIONAL NOTES, THOUGHTS, REFLECTIONS, VIBES AND GRATITUDE:

What are you doing to get closer to your goals, intentions, and wellness? What are the challenges you are facing? What else comes up during your day to reflect on?

MY DAILY VIBE

"When you devote time and energy to noticing, new doors open. Serendipity accelerates, you feel like the universe is conspiring to support you. But really, you're just not limiting yourself."

Date: _____

(MY) WELL-BEING CHECK IN:
How I'm feeling

....
....
....

(MY) GRATITUDE TODAY:
What, who and things I'm grateful for

....
....
....

(MY) INTENTION FOR TODAY:
What I hope/intend to accomplish or even create today?

....
....
....

(MY) GOAL FOR WHAT I'M WORKING ON AND CREATING:

....
....
....

I AM:
My affirmation for today

ADDITIONAL NOTES, THOUGHTS, REFLECTIONS, VIBES AND GRATITUDE:

What are you doing to get closer to your goals, intentions, and wellness? What are the challenges you are facing? What else comes up during your day to reflect on?

MY DAILY VIBE

"When you face difficult times, know that challenges are not sent to destroy you. They're sent to promote, increase and strengthen you."

- JOEL OSTEEN

Date: _____

(MY) WELL-BEING CHECK IN:
How I'm feeling

....
....
....

(MY) GRATITUDE TODAY:
What, who and things I'm grateful for

....
....
....

(MY) INTENTION FOR TODAY:
What I hope/intend to accomplish or even create today?

....
....
....

(MY) GOAL FOR WHAT I'M WORKING ON AND CREATING:

....
....
....

I AM:
My affirmation for today

ADDITIONAL NOTES, THOUGHTS, REFLECTIONS, VIBES AND GRATITUDE:

What are you doing to get closer to your goals, intentions, and wellness? What are the challenges you are facing? What else comes up during your day to reflect on?

MY DAILY VIBE

"When you know yourself you are empowered. When you accept yourself you are invincible."

-TINA LIFFORD

Date: _____

(MY) WELL-BEING CHECK IN:
How I'm feeling

....
....
....

(MY) GRATITUDE TODAY:
What, who and things I'm grateful for

....
....
....

(MY) INTENTION FOR TODAY:
What I hope/intend to accomplish or even create today?

....
....
....

(MY) GOAL FOR WHAT I'M WORKING ON AND CREATING:

....
....
....

I AM:
My affirmation for today

ADDITIONAL NOTES, THOUGHTS, REFLECTIONS, VIBES AND GRATITUDE:

What are you doing to get closer to your goals, intentions, and wellness? What are the challenges you are facing? What else comes up during your day to reflect on?

MY DAILY VIBE

"When you recognize hat you will thrive note in spite of your losses and sorrows, but because of them, that you would not have chosen the things that happened in your life, but you are grateful for them, that you will hold the empty bowls eternally in your hands, but you also have the capacity to fill them. The word for that is healing.""

-CHERYL STRAYED.

Date: _____

(MY) WELL-BEING CHECK IN:
How I'm feeling

....
....
....

(MY) GRATITUDE TODAY:
What, who and things I'm grateful for

....
....
....

(MY) INTENTION FOR TODAY:
What I hope/intend to accomplish or even create today?

....
....
....

(MY) GOAL FOR WHAT I'M WORKING ON AND CREATING:

....
....
....

I AM:
My affirmation for today

ADDITIONAL NOTES, THOUGHTS, REFLECTIONS, VIBES AND GRATITUDE:

What are you doing to get closer to your goals, intentions, and wellness? What are the challenges you are facing? What else comes up during your day to reflect on?

MY DAILY VIBE

"When you start seeing your worth, you'll find it harder to stay around people who don't."

Date: _____

❤️ (MY) WELL-BEING CHECK IN:
How I'm feeling

....
....
....

🙌 (MY) GRATITUDE TODAY:
What, who and things I'm grateful for

....
....
....

📅 (MY) INTENTION FOR TODAY:
What I hope/intend to accomplish or even create today?

....
....
....

🎯 (MY) GOAL FOR WHAT I'M WORKING ON AND CREATING:

....
....
....

💪 I AM:
My affirmation for today

ADDITIONAL NOTES, THOUGHTS, REFLECTIONS, VIBES AND GRATITUDE:

What are you doing to get closer to your goals, intentions, and wellness? What are the challenges you are facing? What else comes up during your day to reflect on?

MY DAILY VIBE

"WHEN YOUR FREQUENCY IS HIGH YOU'RE ABLE TO SEE THE GOOD IN EVERYTHING."

- IAN DAVIS

Date: _____

(MY) WELL-BEING CHECK IN:
How I'm feeling

....
....
....

(MY) GRATITUDE TODAY:
What, who and things I'm grateful for

....
....
....

(MY) INTENTION FOR TODAY:
What I hope/intend to accomplish or even create today?

....
....
....

(MY) GOAL FOR WHAT I'M WORKING ON AND CREATING:

....
....
....

I AM:
My affirmation for today

....

ADDITIONAL NOTES, THOUGHTS, REFLECTIONS, VIBES AND GRATITUDE:

What are you doing to get closer to your goals, intentions, and wellness? What are the challenges you are facing? What else comes up during your day to reflect on?

MY DAILY VIBE

"When your heart is broken, it is most open. When life has crushed your dreams, it has produced a path toward even better ones. Be not discouraged you're built to win."

- ROBIN SHARMA

Date: _____

(MY) WELL-BEING CHECK IN:
How I'm feeling

(MY) GRATITUDE TODAY:
What, who and things I'm grateful for

(MY) INTENTION FOR TODAY:
What I hope/intend to accomplish or even create today?

(MY) GOAL FOR WHAT I'M WORKING ON AND CREATING:

I AM:
My affirmation for today

ADDITIONAL NOTES, THOUGHTS, REFLECTIONS, VIBES AND GRATITUDE:

What are you doing to get closer to your goals, intentions, and wellness? What are the challenges you are facing? What else comes up during your day to reflect on?

MY DAILY VIBE

"Whether its the best of times or the wort of times it's the only time you've got."

- ART BUCHWALD.

Date: _____

(MY) WELL-BEING CHECK IN:
How I'm feeling

....
....
....

(MY) GRATITUDE TODAY:
What, who and things I'm grateful for

....
....
....

(MY) INTENTION FOR TODAY:
What I hope/intend to accomplish or even create today?

....
....
....

(MY) GOAL FOR WHAT I'M WORKING ON AND CREATING:

....
....
....

I AM:
My affirmation for today

ADDITIONAL NOTES, THOUGHTS, REFLECTIONS, VIBES AND GRATITUDE:

What are you doing to get closer to your goals, intentions, and wellness? What are the challenges you are facing? What else comes up during your day to reflect on?

MY DAILY VIBE

"Who looks outside, dreams; who looks inside, awakes."
- CARL JUNG

Date: _____

♥ (MY) WELL-BEING CHECK IN:
How I'm feeling

....
....
....

🙌 (MY) GRATITUDE TODAY:
What, who and things I'm grateful for

....
....
....

📅 (MY) INTENTION FOR TODAY:
What I hope/intend to accomplish or even create today?

....
....
....

🎯 (MY) GOAL FOR WHAT I'M WORKING ON AND CREATING:

....
....
....

💪 I AM:
My affirmation for today

ADDITIONAL NOTES, THOUGHTS, REFLECTIONS, VIBES AND GRATITUDE:

What are you doing to get closer to your goals, intentions, and wellness? What are the challenges you are facing? What else comes up during your day to reflect on?

MY DAILY VIBE

*"Will it be easy? Nope
Worth it? Absolutely."*

Date: _____

(MY) WELL-BEING CHECK IN:
How I'm feeling

....
....
....

(MY) GRATITUDE TODAY:
What, who and things I'm grateful for

....
....
....

(MY) INTENTION FOR TODAY:
What I hope/intend to accomplish or even create today?

....
....
....

(MY) GOAL FOR WHAT I'M WORKING ON AND CREATING:

....
....
....

I AM:
My affirmation for today

ADDITIONAL NOTES, THOUGHTS, REFLECTIONS, VIBES AND GRATITUDE:

What are you doing to get closer to your goals, intentions, and wellness? What are the challenges you are facing? What else comes up during your day to reflect on?

MY DAILY VIBE

"Winners never quit and quitters never win."
- VINCE LOMBARDI

Date: _____

(MY) WELL-BEING CHECK IN:
How I'm feeling

....
....
....

(MY) GRATITUDE TODAY:
What, who and things I'm grateful for

....
....
....

(MY) INTENTION FOR TODAY:
What I hope/intend to accomplish or even create today?

....
....
....

(MY) GOAL FOR WHAT I'M WORKING ON AND CREATING:

....
....
....

I AM:
My affirmation for today

ADDITIONAL NOTES, THOUGHTS, REFLECTIONS, VIBES AND GRATITUDE:

What are you doing to get closer to your goals, intentions, and wellness? What are the challenges you are facing? What else comes up during your day to reflect on?

MY DAILY VIBE

"Winning means you're willing to go longer, work harder and give more than anyone else."

- VINCE LOMBARDI

Date: _____

(MY) WELL-BEING CHECK IN:
How I'm feeling

....
....
....

(MY) GRATITUDE TODAY:
What, who and things I'm grateful for

....
....
....

(MY) INTENTION FOR TODAY:
What I hope/intend to accomplish or even create today?

....
....
....

(MY) GOAL FOR WHAT I'M WORKING ON AND CREATING:

....
....
....

I AM:
My affirmation for today

ADDITIONAL NOTES, THOUGHTS, REFLECTIONS, VIBES AND GRATITUDE:

What are you doing to get closer to your goals, intentions, and wellness? What are the challenges you are facing? What else comes up during your day to reflect on?

MY DAILY VIBE

"Worrying won't stop the bad stuff from happening it just stops you from enjoying the good."

Date: _____

♡ (MY) WELL-BEING CHECK IN:
How I'm feeling

....
....
....

✋ (MY) GRATITUDE TODAY:
What, who and things I'm grateful for

....
....
....

📅 (MY) INTENTION FOR TODAY:
What I hope/intend to accomplish or even create today?

....
....
....

🎯 (MY) GOAL FOR WHAT I'M WORKING ON AND CREATING:

....
....
....

💪 I AM:
My affirmation for today

ADDITIONAL NOTES, THOUGHTS, REFLECTIONS, VIBES AND GRATITUDE:

What are you doing to get closer to your goals, intentions, and wellness? What are the challenges you are facing? What else comes up during your day to reflect on?

MY DAILY VIBE

"YOU ARE A CONSTANT, BOUNTIFUL FORCE WITHOUT END. MAY YOU USE YOUR SUPPLY TO BE WELL. BE PROSPEROUS BE SAFE AND BE HAPPY. MAY IT BE SO."

- IAN DAVIS

Date: _____

(MY) WELL-BEING CHECK IN:
How I'm feeling

(MY) GRATITUDE TODAY:
What, who and things I'm grateful for

(MY) INTENTION FOR TODAY:
What I hope/intend to accomplish or even create today?

(MY) GOAL FOR WHAT I'M WORKING ON AND CREATING:

I AM:
My affirmation for today

ADDITIONAL NOTES, THOUGHTS, REFLECTIONS, VIBES AND GRATITUDE:

What are you doing to get closer to your goals, intentions, and wellness? What are the challenges you are facing? What else comes up during your day to reflect on?

MY DAILY VIBE

"You are a vibrational being. The universe knows how you truly feel & what you truly believe based on your vibrational frequency. You will attract to you whatever you're in harmonious vibration with. You are in control of that."

Date: _____

(MY) WELL-BEING CHECK IN:
How I'm feeling

....
....
....

(MY) GRATITUDE TODAY:
What, who and things I'm grateful for

....
....
....

(MY) INTENTION FOR TODAY:
What I hope/intend to accomplish or even create today?

....
....
....

(MY) GOAL FOR WHAT I'M WORKING ON AND CREATING:

....
....
....

I AM:
My affirmation for today

ADDITIONAL NOTES, THOUGHTS, REFLECTIONS, VIBES AND GRATITUDE:

What are you doing to get closer to your goals, intentions, and wellness? What are the challenges you are facing? What else comes up during your day to reflect on?

MY DAILY VIBE

"You are awareness. Awareness is another name for you. Since you are awareness there is no need to attain or cultivate it."

— RAMANA MAHARSHI

Date: _____

(MY) WELL-BEING CHECK IN:
How I'm feeling

....
....
....

(MY) GRATITUDE TODAY:
What, who and things I'm grateful for

....
....
....

(MY) INTENTION FOR TODAY:
What I hope/intend to accomplish or even create today?

....
....
....

(MY) GOAL FOR WHAT I'M WORKING ON AND CREATING:

....
....
....

I AM:
My affirmation for today

....

ADDITIONAL NOTES, THOUGHTS, REFLECTIONS, VIBES AND GRATITUDE:

What are you doing to get closer to your goals, intentions, and wellness? What are the challenges you are facing? What else comes up during your day to reflect on?

MY DAILY VIBE

"You are braver than you believe, smarter than you seem, and stronger than you think."

- WINNIE THE POOH

Date: _____

(MY) WELL-BEING CHECK IN:
How I'm feeling

....
....
....

(MY) GRATITUDE TODAY:
What, who and things I'm grateful for

....
....
....

(MY) INTENTION FOR TODAY:
What I hope/intend to accomplish or even create today?

....
....
....

(MY) GOAL FOR WHAT I'M WORKING ON AND CREATING:

....
....
....

I AM:
My affirmation for today

ADDITIONAL NOTES, THOUGHTS, REFLECTIONS, VIBES AND GRATITUDE:

What are you doing to get closer to your goals, intentions, and wellness? What are the challenges you are facing? What else comes up during your day to reflect on?

START EACH DAY LIKE IT'S YOUR BIRTHDAY!

– UNKNOWN

MY TARGETS FOR THE MONTH OF: _____

NOTES

MY DAILY VIBE

"You are infinite. May you become what you believe. May you get closer to your highest and best self. May your day be Great, good and abundant. Smile and deep inhale, exhale and release."

— IAN DAVIS

Date: _____

(MY) WELL-BEING CHECK IN:
How I'm feeling

....
....
....

(MY) GRATITUDE TODAY:
What, who and things I'm grateful for

....
....
....

(MY) INTENTION FOR TODAY:
What I hope/intend to accomplish or even create today?

....
....
....

(MY) GOAL FOR WHAT I'M WORKING ON AND CREATING:

....
....
....

I AM:
My affirmation for today

ADDITIONAL NOTES, THOUGHTS, REFLECTIONS, VIBES AND GRATITUDE:

What are you doing to get closer to your goals, intentions, and wellness? What are the challenges you are facing? What else comes up during your day to reflect on?

MY DAILY VIBE

"YOU ARE INFINITE. THERE IS NO LIMIT TO THE ABUNDANCE YOU HAVE AND MAY CREATE FROM WITHIN. THERE ARE MIRACLES WAITING FOR YOU. YOU ARE CONFIDENT, YOU ARE SECURE, YOU ARE BLESSED, YOU ARE LOVED."

- IAN DAVIS

Date: _____

(MY) WELL-BEING CHECK IN:
How I'm feeling

....
....
....

(MY) GRATITUDE TODAY:
What, who and things I'm grateful for

....
....
....

(MY) INTENTION FOR TODAY:
What I hope/intend to accomplish or even create today?

....
....
....

(MY) GOAL FOR WHAT I'M WORKING ON AND CREATING:

....
....
....

I AM:
My affirmation for today

ADDITIONAL NOTES, THOUGHTS, REFLECTIONS, VIBES AND GRATITUDE:

What are you doing to get closer to your goals, intentions, and wellness? What are the challenges you are facing? What else comes up during your day to reflect on?

MY DAILY VIBE

"YOU ARE LIFE YOU ARE LOVE. YOU ARE LIGHT. YOU ARE ALL KNOWLEDGE, ALL WISDOM, ALL POWER. GREAT AND INFINITE AND ABUNDANT ARE YOU. MAY YOU USE ALL THAT YOU ARE AND HAVE TO BECOME WHAT YOU BELIEVE."

- IAN DAVIS

Date: _____

(MY) WELL-BEING CHECK IN:
How I'm feeling

(MY) GRATITUDE TODAY:
What, who and things I'm grateful for

(MY) INTENTION FOR TODAY:
What I hope/intend to accomplish or even create today?

(MY) GOAL FOR WHAT I'M WORKING ON AND CREATING:

I AM:
My affirmation for today

ADDITIONAL NOTES, THOUGHTS, REFLECTIONS, VIBES AND GRATITUDE:

What are you doing to get closer to your goals, intentions, and wellness? What are the challenges you are facing? What else comes up during your day to reflect on?

MY DAILY VIBE

"You are love and loved. You are an expression of love and the source of love is deep within you. You are blessed. You are whole. You are a gift and full of infinite possibilities. May you move toward love."

- IAN DAVIS

Date: _____

(MY) WELL-BEING CHECK IN:
How I'm feeling

....
....
....

(MY) GRATITUDE TODAY:
What, who and things I'm grateful for

....
....
....

(MY) INTENTION FOR TODAY:
What I hope/intend to accomplish or even create today?

....
....
....

(MY) GOAL FOR WHAT I'M WORKING ON AND CREATING:

....
....
....

I AM:
My affirmation for today

ADDITIONAL NOTES, THOUGHTS, REFLECTIONS, VIBES AND GRATITUDE:

What are you doing to get closer to your goals, intentions, and wellness? What are the challenges you are facing? What else comes up during your day to reflect on?

MY DAILY VIBE

"You are never too old to set another goal or to dream a new dream."
- C.S. LEWIS

Date: _____

❤️ (MY) WELL-BEING CHECK IN:
How I'm feeling

....
....
....

🙌 (MY) GRATITUDE TODAY:
What, who and things I'm grateful for

....
....
....

📅 (MY) INTENTION FOR TODAY:
What I hope/intend to accomplish or even create today?

....
....
....

🎯 (MY) GOAL FOR WHAT I'M WORKING ON AND CREATING:

....
....
....

💪 I AM:
My affirmation for today

ADDITIONAL NOTES, THOUGHTS, REFLECTIONS, VIBES AND GRATITUDE:

What are you doing to get closer to your goals, intentions, and wellness? What are the challenges you are facing? What else comes up during your day to reflect on?

MY DAILY VIBE

"You attract what you fear, feel and think."

Date: _____

♥ (MY) WELL-BEING CHECK IN:
How I'm feeling

....
....
....

🙌 (MY) GRATITUDE TODAY:
What, who and things I'm grateful for

....
....
....

📅 (MY) INTENTION FOR TODAY:
What I hope/intend to accomplish or even create today?

....
....
....

🎯 (MY) GOAL FOR WHAT I'M WORKING ON AND CREATING:

....
....
....

💪 I AM:
My affirmation for today

....

ADDITIONAL NOTES, THOUGHTS, REFLECTIONS, VIBES AND GRATITUDE:

What are you doing to get closer to your goals, intentions, and wellness? What are the challenges you are facing? What else comes up during your day to reflect on?

MY DAILY VIBE

"You can have results or excuses. Not both."
- ARNOLD SCHWARZENEGGE

Date: _____

(MY) WELL-BEING CHECK IN:
How I'm feeling

....
....
....

(MY) GRATITUDE TODAY:
What, who and things I'm grateful for

....
....
....

(MY) INTENTION FOR TODAY:
What I hope/intend to accomplish or even create today?

....
....
....

(MY) GOAL FOR WHAT I'M WORKING ON AND CREATING:

....
....
....

I AM:
My affirmation for today

ADDITIONAL NOTES, THOUGHTS, REFLECTIONS, VIBES AND GRATITUDE:

What are you doing to get closer to your goals, intentions, and wellness? What are the challenges you are facing? What else comes up during your day to reflect on?

MY DAILY VIBE

"You can't live a positive life with a negative mind."

Date: _____

♡ (MY) WELL-BEING CHECK IN:
How I'm feeling

....
....
....

👐 (MY) GRATITUDE TODAY:
What, who and things I'm grateful for

....
....
....

📅 (MY) INTENTION FOR TODAY:
What I hope/intend to accomplish or even create today?

....
....
....

🎯 (MY) GOAL FOR WHAT I'M WORKING ON AND CREATING:

....
....
....

💪 I AM:
My affirmation for today

....

ADDITIONAL NOTES, THOUGHTS, REFLECTIONS, VIBES AND GRATITUDE:

What are you doing to get closer to your goals, intentions, and wellness? What are the challenges you are facing? What else comes up during your day to reflect on?

MY DAILY VIBE

"You cannot find peace by avoiding life."

Date: _____

♥ (MY) WELL-BEING CHECK IN:
How I'm feeling

....
....
....

🙌 (MY) GRATITUDE TODAY:
What, who and things I'm grateful for

....
....
....

📅 (MY) INTENTION FOR TODAY:
What I hope/intend to accomplish or even create today?

....
....
....

🎯 (MY) GOAL FOR WHAT I'M WORKING ON AND CREATING:

....
....
....

💪 I AM:
My affirmation for today

....

ADDITIONAL NOTES, THOUGHTS, REFLECTIONS, VIBES AND GRATITUDE:

What are you doing to get closer to your goals, intentions, and wellness? What are the challenges you are facing? What else comes up during your day to reflect on?

MY DAILY VIBE

"You create your own opportunities."

Date: _____

❤️ (MY) WELL-BEING CHECK IN:
How I'm feeling

....
....
....

🙌 (MY) GRATITUDE TODAY:
What, who and things I'm grateful for

....
....
....

📅 (MY) INTENTION FOR TODAY:
What I hope/intend to accomplish or even create today?

....
....
....

🎯 (MY) GOAL FOR WHAT I'M WORKING ON AND CREATING:

....
....
....

💪 I AM:
My affirmation for today

ADDITIONAL NOTES, THOUGHTS, REFLECTIONS, VIBES AND GRATITUDE:

What are you doing to get closer to your goals, intentions, and wellness? What are the challenges you are facing? What else comes up during your day to reflect on?

MY DAILY VIBE

"You create your reality every second of your life. May you be constantly guided and boldly empowered to receive a full measure of infinite good. Deep inhale, exhale and release, a smile."

- IAN DAVIS

Date: _____

(MY) WELL-BEING CHECK IN:
How I'm feeling

....
....
....

(MY) GRATITUDE TODAY:
What, who and things I'm grateful for

....
....
....

(MY) INTENTION FOR TODAY:
What I hope/intend to accomplish or even create today?

....
....
....

(MY) GOAL FOR WHAT I'M WORKING ON AND CREATING:

....
....
....

I AM:
My affirmation for today

ADDITIONAL NOTES, THOUGHTS, REFLECTIONS, VIBES AND GRATITUDE:

What are you doing to get closer to your goals, intentions, and wellness? What are the challenges you are facing? What else comes up during your day to reflect on?

MY DAILY VIBE

"You didn't come this far to only come this far."

Date: _____

♥ (MY) WELL-BEING CHECK IN:
How I'm feeling

....
....
....

🙌 (MY) GRATITUDE TODAY:
What, who and things I'm grateful for

....
....
....

📅 (MY) INTENTION FOR TODAY:
What I hope/intend to accomplish or even create today?

....
....
....

🎯 (MY) GOAL FOR WHAT I'M WORKING ON AND CREATING:

....
....
....

💪 I AM:
My affirmation for today

....

ADDITIONAL NOTES, THOUGHTS, REFLECTIONS, VIBES AND GRATITUDE:

What are you doing to get closer to your goals, intentions, and wellness? What are the challenges you are facing? What else comes up during your day to reflect on?

MY DAILY VIBE

"You don't get what you wish for. You get what you work for."

Date: _____

(MY) WELL-BEING CHECK IN:
How I'm feeling

....
....
....

(MY) GRATITUDE TODAY:
What, who and things I'm grateful for

....
....
....

(MY) INTENTION FOR TODAY:
What I hope/intend to accomplish or even create today?

....
....
....

(MY) GOAL FOR WHAT I'M WORKING ON AND CREATING:

....
....
....

I AM:
My affirmation for today

ADDITIONAL NOTES, THOUGHTS, REFLECTIONS, VIBES AND GRATITUDE:

What are you doing to get closer to your goals, intentions, and wellness? What are the challenges you are facing? What else comes up during your day to reflect on?

MY DAILY VIBE

"You have creative power to rise above limitation. May you live intentionally. May you live toward and in your higher potential."

- IAN DAVIS

Date: _____

(MY) WELL-BEING CHECK IN:
How I'm feeling

(MY) GRATITUDE TODAY:
What, who and things I'm grateful for

(MY) INTENTION FOR TODAY:
What I hope/intend to accomplish or even create today?

(MY) GOAL FOR WHAT I'M WORKING ON AND CREATING:

I AM:
My affirmation for today

ADDITIONAL NOTES, THOUGHTS, REFLECTIONS, VIBES AND GRATITUDE:

What are you doing to get closer to your goals, intentions, and wellness? What are the challenges you are facing? What else comes up during your day to reflect on?

MY DAILY VIBE

"You have strength. You are a conqueror. You can live in and have joy. May you be mindful, present and continue to help yourself. Trust your power."

- IAN DAVIS

Date: _____

(MY) WELL-BEING CHECK IN:
How I'm feeling

(MY) GRATITUDE TODAY:
What, who and things I'm grateful for

(MY) INTENTION FOR TODAY:
What I hope/intend to accomplish or even create today?

(MY) GOAL FOR WHAT I'M WORKING ON AND CREATING:

I AM:
My affirmation for today

ADDITIONAL NOTES, THOUGHTS, REFLECTIONS, VIBES AND GRATITUDE:

What are you doing to get closer to your goals, intentions, and wellness? What are the challenges you are facing? What else comes up during your day to reflect on?

MY DAILY VIBE

"You have to put up with the risk of being misunderstood if you are going to try to communicate. But it's worth being a public fool if that's all you can be in order to communicate yourself."

– EDIE SEDGWICK

Date: _____

(MY) WELL-BEING CHECK IN:
How I'm feeling

....
....
....

(MY) GRATITUDE TODAY:
What, who and things I'm grateful for

....
....
....

(MY) INTENTION FOR TODAY:
What I hope/intend to accomplish or even create today?

....
....
....

(MY) GOAL FOR WHAT I'M WORKING ON AND CREATING:

....
....
....

I AM:
My affirmation for today

ADDITIONAL NOTES, THOUGHTS, REFLECTIONS, VIBES AND GRATITUDE:

What are you doing to get closer to your goals, intentions, and wellness? What are the challenges you are facing? What else comes up during your day to reflect on?

MY DAILY VIBE

"You must believe you are the best and then make sure that you are."
- BILL SHANKLY

Date: _____

(MY) WELL-BEING CHECK IN:
How I'm feeling

....
....
....

(MY) GRATITUDE TODAY:
What, who and things I'm grateful for

....
....
....

(MY) INTENTION FOR TODAY:
What I hope/intend to accomplish or even create today?

....
....
....

(MY) GOAL FOR WHAT I'M WORKING ON AND CREATING:

....
....
....

I AM:
My affirmation for today

ADDITIONAL NOTES, THOUGHTS, REFLECTIONS, VIBES AND GRATITUDE:

What are you doing to get closer to your goals, intentions, and wellness? What are the challenges you are facing? What else comes up during your day to reflect on?

MY DAILY VIBE

"You must not let you life run in the ordinary way; do something that nobody else has done, something that will dazzle the word. Show that God's creative principle works in you."

- YOGANANDA

Date: _____

(MY) WELL-BEING CHECK IN:
How I'm feeling

....
....
....

(MY) GRATITUDE TODAY:
What, who and things I'm grateful for

....
....
....

(MY) INTENTION FOR TODAY:
What I hope/intend to accomplish or even create today?

....
....
....

(MY) GOAL FOR WHAT I'M WORKING ON AND CREATING:

....
....
....

I AM:
My affirmation for today

ADDITIONAL NOTES, THOUGHTS, REFLECTIONS, VIBES AND GRATITUDE:

What are you doing to get closer to your goals, intentions, and wellness? What are the challenges you are facing? What else comes up during your day to reflect on?

MY DAILY VIBE

"You only get one life. It's actually your duty to love it as fully as possible."
- JOJO MOYES

Date: _____

(MY) WELL-BEING CHECK IN:
How I'm feeling

....
....
....

(MY) GRATITUDE TODAY:
What, who and things I'm grateful for

....
....
....

(MY) INTENTION FOR TODAY:
What I hope/intend to accomplish or even create today?

....
....
....

(MY) GOAL FOR WHAT I'M WORKING ON AND CREATING:

....
....
....

I AM:
My affirmation for today

ADDITIONAL NOTES, THOUGHTS, REFLECTIONS, VIBES AND GRATITUDE:

What are you doing to get closer to your goals, intentions, and wellness? What are the challenges you are facing? What else comes up during your day to reflect on?

MY DAILY VIBE

"You're allowed to scream, you're allowed to cry, but do not give up."

Date: _____

(MY) WELL-BEING CHECK IN:
How I'm feeling

....
....
....

(MY) GRATITUDE TODAY:
What, who and things I'm grateful for

....
....
....

(MY) INTENTION FOR TODAY:
What I hope/intend to accomplish or even create today?

....
....
....

(MY) GOAL FOR WHAT I'M WORKING ON AND CREATING:

....
....
....

I AM:
My affirmation for today

ADDITIONAL NOTES, THOUGHTS, REFLECTIONS, VIBES AND GRATITUDE:

What are you doing to get closer to your goals, intentions, and wellness? What are the challenges you are facing? What else comes up during your day to reflect on?

MY DAILY VIBE

"You're over here doubting yourself whist so many people are intimidated by your potential."

Date: _____

(MY) WELL-BEING CHECK IN:
How I'm feeling

....
....
....

(MY) GRATITUDE TODAY:
What, who and things I'm grateful for

....
....
....

(MY) INTENTION FOR TODAY:
What I hope/intend to accomplish or even create today?

....
....
....

(MY) GOAL FOR WHAT I'M WORKING ON AND CREATING:

....
....
....

I AM:
My affirmation for today

ADDITIONAL NOTES, THOUGHTS, REFLECTIONS, VIBES AND GRATITUDE:

What are you doing to get closer to your goals, intentions, and wellness? What are the challenges you are facing? What else comes up during your day to reflect on?

MY DAILY VIBE

"You're picky about the car you drive. You're picky about what you wear. You're picky about what you put in your mouth, be pickier about what you think."

- ABRAHAM HICKS

Date: _____

(MY) WELL-BEING CHECK IN:
How I'm feeling

(MY) GRATITUDE TODAY:
What, who and things I'm grateful for

(MY) INTENTION FOR TODAY:
What I hope/intend to accomplish or even create today?

(MY) GOAL FOR WHAT I'M WORKING ON AND CREATING:

I AM:
My affirmation for today

ADDITIONAL NOTES, THOUGHTS, REFLECTIONS, VIBES AND GRATITUDE:

What are you doing to get closer to your goals, intentions, and wellness? What are the challenges you are facing? What else comes up during your day to reflect on?

MY DAILY VIBE

"You're in the drivers seat, Shift your mind-set! Feel empowered, engaged, and positive. Call in your abundant birthright. May you place no limits on your thinking. May you be excited about the challenges and growth ahead. Breathe in deeply and exhale evenly."

- IAN DAVIS

Date: _____

(MY) WELL-BEING CHECK IN:
How I'm feeling

....
....
....

(MY) GRATITUDE TODAY:
What, who and things I'm grateful for

....
....
....

(MY) INTENTION FOR TODAY:
What I hope/intend to accomplish or even create today?

....
....
....

(MY) GOAL FOR WHAT I'M WORKING ON AND CREATING:

....
....
....

I AM:
My affirmation for today

ADDITIONAL NOTES, THOUGHTS, REFLECTIONS, VIBES AND GRATITUDE:

What are you doing to get closer to your goals, intentions, and wellness? What are the challenges you are facing? What else comes up during your day to reflect on?

MY DAILY VIBE

"Your level of success is determined by your level of discipline and perseverance."

- VELUSAMY DHAMODARAN

Date: _____

(MY) WELL-BEING CHECK IN:
How I'm feeling

....
....
....

(MY) GRATITUDE TODAY:
What, who and things I'm grateful for

....
....
....

(MY) INTENTION FOR TODAY:
What I hope/intend to accomplish or even create today?

....
....
....

(MY) GOAL FOR WHAT I'M WORKING ON AND CREATING:

....
....
....

I AM:
My affirmation for today

ADDITIONAL NOTES, THOUGHTS, REFLECTIONS, VIBES AND GRATITUDE:

What are you doing to get closer to your goals, intentions, and wellness? What are the challenges you are facing? What else comes up during your day to reflect on?

MY DAILY VIBE

"Your mind is a magnet. If you think of blessings you attract blessings; and if you think of problems you attract problems. Always cultivate good thoughts and always remain positive ad optimistic. We get what we think, so think positive, life will be automatically positive."

Date: _____

(MY) WELL-BEING CHECK IN:
How I'm feeling

....
....
....

(MY) GRATITUDE TODAY:
What, who and things I'm grateful for

....
....
....

(MY) INTENTION FOR TODAY:
What I hope/intend to accomplish or even create today?

....
....
....

(MY) GOAL FOR WHAT I'M WORKING ON AND CREATING:

....
....
....

I AM:
My affirmation for today

ADDITIONAL NOTES, THOUGHTS, REFLECTIONS, VIBES AND GRATITUDE:

What are you doing to get closer to your goals, intentions, and wellness? What are the challenges you are facing? What else comes up during your day to reflect on?

MY DAILY VIBE

"Your time is coming. The right people, opportunities, and breaks are headed your way. Please have faith and don't give up. It's all coming."

— NICOLE ADDISON

Date: _____

(MY) WELL-BEING CHECK IN:
How I'm feeling

....
....
....

(MY) GRATITUDE TODAY:
What, who and things I'm grateful for

....
....
....

(MY) INTENTION FOR TODAY:
What I hope/intend to accomplish or even create today?

....
....
....

(MY) GOAL FOR WHAT I'M WORKING ON AND CREATING:

....
....
....

I AM:
My affirmation for today

ADDITIONAL NOTES, THOUGHTS, REFLECTIONS, VIBES AND GRATITUDE:

What are you doing to get closer to your goals, intentions, and wellness? What are the challenges you are facing? What else comes up during your day to reflect on?

MY DAILY VIBE

"Your time is precious. Don't waste it on anyone who doesn't realize that you are too."

- ROBERT TEW

Date: _____

(MY) WELL-BEING CHECK IN:
How I'm feeling

....
....
....

(MY) GRATITUDE TODAY:
What, who and things I'm grateful for

....
....
....

(MY) INTENTION FOR TODAY:
What I hope/intend to accomplish or even create today?

....
....
....

(MY) GOAL FOR WHAT I'M WORKING ON AND CREATING:

....
....
....

I AM:
My affirmation for today

ADDITIONAL NOTES, THOUGHTS, REFLECTIONS, VIBES AND GRATITUDE:

What are you doing to get closer to your goals, intentions, and wellness? What are the challenges you are facing? What else comes up during your day to reflect on?

MY DAILY VIBE

"Your true power comes from within. May you realize how infinite you are. May you be mindful, present and go within to help yourself. May you live your power. Smile and inhale, your power, exhale and release."

- IAN DAVIS

Date: _____

(MY) WELL-BEING CHECK IN:
How I'm feeling

....
....
....

(MY) GRATITUDE TODAY:
What, who and things I'm grateful for

....
....
....

(MY) INTENTION FOR TODAY:
What I hope/intend to accomplish or even create today?

....
....
....

(MY) GOAL FOR WHAT I'M WORKING ON AND CREATING:

....
....
....

I AM:
My affirmation for today

ADDITIONAL NOTES, THOUGHTS, REFLECTIONS, VIBES AND GRATITUDE:

What are you doing to get closer to your goals, intentions, and wellness? What are the challenges you are facing? What else comes up during your day to reflect on?

....
....
....
....
....
....
....
....
....
....
....
....
....
....
....
....
....
....
....
....
....
....
....
....
....
....
....

MY DAILY VIBE

"Your vibe attracts your tribe."
- MARLI WILLIAMS

Date: _____

(MY) WELL-BEING CHECK IN:
How I'm feeling

_____
_____
_____

(MY) GRATITUDE TODAY:
What, who and things I'm grateful for

_____
_____
_____

(MY) INTENTION FOR TODAY:
What I hope/intend to accomplish or even create today?

_____
_____
_____

(MY) GOAL FOR WHAT I'M WORKING ON AND CREATING:

_____
_____
_____

I AM:
My affirmation for today

ADDITIONAL NOTES, THOUGHTS, REFLECTIONS, VIBES AND GRATITUDE:

What are you doing to get closer to your goals, intentions, and wellness? What are the challenges you are facing? What else comes up during your day to reflect on?

MY DAILY VIBE

"3 Simple rules in life:
1. if you do not go after what you want you will never have it.
2. If you don't ask, the answer will always be no.
3. If you do not step forward, you will always be in the same place."

- MARLI WILLIAMS

Date: _____

(MY) WELL-BEING CHECK IN:
How I'm feeling

(MY) GRATITUDE TODAY:
What, who and things I'm grateful for

(MY) INTENTION FOR TODAY:
What I hope/intend to accomplish or even create today?

(MY) GOAL FOR WHAT I'M WORKING ON AND CREATING:

I AM:
My affirmation for today

ADDITIONAL NOTES, THOUGHTS, REFLECTIONS, VIBES AND GRATITUDE:

What are you doing to get closer to your goals, intentions, and wellness? What are the challenges you are facing? What else comes up during your day to reflect on?

MY DAILY VIBE

"Act without doing; work without effort. Think of the small as large and the few as many. Confront the difficult while it is still easy; Accomplish the great task by a series of small acts."

- LAO TZU

Date: _____

(MY) WELL-BEING CHECK IN:
How I'm feeling

....
....
....

(MY) GRATITUDE TODAY:
What, who and things I'm grateful for

....
....
....

(MY) INTENTION FOR TODAY:
What I hope/intend to accomplish or even create today?

....
....
....

(MY) GOAL FOR WHAT I'M WORKING ON AND CREATING:

....
....
....

I AM:
My affirmation for today

ADDITIONAL NOTES, THOUGHTS, REFLECTIONS, VIBES AND GRATITUDE:

What are you doing to get closer to your goals, intentions, and wellness? What are the challenges you are facing? What else comes up during your day to reflect on?

MY DAILY VIBE

"Be a wolf. Be a Lion. Set Goals. Smash Them. Be Stronger. Be Better. Show people who you are. Never Apologize for being awesome. Stay Positive. Stay the Course."

Date: _____

(MY) WELL-BEING CHECK IN:
How I'm feeling

....
....
....

(MY) GRATITUDE TODAY:
What, who and things I'm grateful for

....
....
....

(MY) INTENTION FOR TODAY:
What I hope/intend to accomplish or even create today?

....
....
....

(MY) GOAL FOR WHAT I'M WORKING ON AND CREATING:

....
....
....

I AM:
My affirmation for today

ADDITIONAL NOTES, THOUGHTS, REFLECTIONS, VIBES AND GRATITUDE:

What are you doing to get closer to your goals, intentions, and wellness? What are the challenges you are facing? What else comes up during your day to reflect on?

MY DAILY VIBE

Be kind Work Hard Stay Humble
Smile often keep honest Stay loyal
travel when possible never stop learning
be thankful always and learn

Date: _____

(MY) WELL-BEING CHECK IN:
How I'm feeling

....
....
....

(MY) GRATITUDE TODAY:
What, who and things I'm grateful for

....
....
....

(MY) INTENTION FOR TODAY:
What I hope/intend to accomplish or even create today?

....
....
....

(MY) GOAL FOR WHAT I'M WORKING ON AND CREATING:

....
....
....

I AM:
My affirmation for today

ADDITIONAL NOTES, THOUGHTS, REFLECTIONS, VIBES AND GRATITUDE:

What are you doing to get closer to your goals, intentions, and wellness? What are the challenges you are facing? What else comes up during your day to reflect on?

MY DAILY VIBE

Before you pray – Believe Before you speak – Listen
Before you spend – Earn Before you write – think
Before you quit – Try Before you die – Live.

Date: _____

(MY) WELL-BEING CHECK IN:
How I'm feeling

....
....
....

(MY) GRATITUDE TODAY:
What, who and things I'm grateful for

....
....
....

(MY) INTENTION FOR TODAY:
What I hope/intend to accomplish or even create today?

....
....
....

(MY) GOAL FOR WHAT I'M WORKING ON AND CREATING:

....
....
....

I AM:
My affirmation for today

ADDITIONAL NOTES, THOUGHTS, REFLECTIONS, VIBES AND GRATITUDE:

What are you doing to get closer to your goals, intentions, and wellness? What are the challenges you are facing? What else comes up during your day to reflect on?

MY DAILY VIBE

Don't place limits on your thinking. You are whole, Your are infinite. You are divine. You are capable of any and everything. Awareness has the Power to heal and transform your life. May you be mindful, present, go within and continue to help yourself. May you stay aware. Breathe in deeply and exhale evenly.

Date: _____

(MY) WELL-BEING CHECK IN:
How I'm feeling

....
....
....

(MY) GRATITUDE TODAY:
What, who and things I'm grateful for

....
....
....

(MY) INTENTION FOR TODAY:
What I hope/intend to accomplish or even create today?

....
....
....

(MY) GOAL FOR WHAT I'M WORKING ON AND CREATING:

....
....
....

I AM:
My affirmation for today

ADDITIONAL NOTES, THOUGHTS, REFLECTIONS, VIBES AND GRATITUDE:

What are you doing to get closer to your goals, intentions, and wellness? What are the challenges you are facing? What else comes up during your day to reflect on?

MY DAILY VIBE

"Ego seeks to serve itself, Soul seeks to serve others, Ego seeks outward recognition, Soul seeks inner authenticity, Ego sees life as a competition, Soul sees life as a gift, Ego seeks to preserve self, Soul seeks to preserve others, Ego looks outwards, Soul looks inward, Ego feels lack, Soul feels abundance, Ego is mortal, Soul is eternal, Ego is drawn to lust, Soul is drawn to love, Ego seeks wisdom, Soul is wisdom, Ego enjoys the prize, Soul enjoys the journey, Ego is cause to pain, Soul is cause of healing, Ego rejects God, Soul embraces God, Ego is me, Soul is we."

— FRANK ZAPPA

Date: _____

(MY) WELL-BEING CHECK IN:
How I'm feeling

....
....
....

(MY) GRATITUDE TODAY:
What, who and things I'm grateful for

....
....
....

(MY) INTENTION FOR TODAY:
What I hope/intend to accomplish or even create today?

....
....
....

(MY) GOAL FOR WHAT I'M WORKING ON AND CREATING:

....
....
....

I AM:
My affirmation for today

ADDITIONAL NOTES, THOUGHTS, REFLECTIONS, VIBES AND GRATITUDE:

What are you doing to get closer to your goals, intentions, and wellness? What are the challenges you are facing? What else comes up during your day to reflect on?

MY DAILY VIBE

Sometimes in life, things get messed up, people over-think, over-analyze, and assume. It's human nature though. We aren't perfect and I'm learning this more and more each day. Everybody's beautiful, everybody's flawed and everybody deserves second chances. I don't care what you did, how bad you did it or anything. Sometimes we just weren't ready to make it right the first time. We're only human, remember that.

Date: _____

(MY) WELL-BEING CHECK IN:
How I'm feeling

....
....
....

(MY) GRATITUDE TODAY:
What, who and things I'm grateful for

....
....
....

(MY) INTENTION FOR TODAY:
What I hope/intend to accomplish or even create today?

....
....
....

(MY) GOAL FOR WHAT I'M WORKING ON AND CREATING:

....
....
....

I AM:
My affirmation for today

ADDITIONAL NOTES, THOUGHTS, REFLECTIONS, VIBES AND GRATITUDE:

What are you doing to get closer to your goals, intentions, and wellness? What are the challenges you are facing? What else comes up during your day to reflect on?

MY DAILY VIBE

"The power of of the spirit that is in and flows through you is unlimited. Tap in! May you realize your wholeness. May you be mindful, present, go within and continue to help yourself. Deep inhale, exhale and release. May it be so."

- FRANK ZAPPA

Date: _____

(MY) WELL-BEING CHECK IN:
How I'm feeling

....
....
....

(MY) GRATITUDE TODAY:
What, who and things I'm grateful for

....
....
....

(MY) INTENTION FOR TODAY:
What I hope/intend to accomplish or even create today?

....
....
....

(MY) GOAL FOR WHAT I'M WORKING ON AND CREATING:

....
....
....

I AM:
My affirmation for today

ADDITIONAL NOTES, THOUGHTS, REFLECTIONS, VIBES AND GRATITUDE:

What are you doing to get closer to your goals, intentions, and wellness? What are the challenges you are facing? What else comes up during your day to reflect on?

MY DAILY VIBE

"There is no such thing as "going back to square one." Even if you feel like you're having to start over, you are trying again with more knowledge, strength & power than you had before. Your journey was never over, it was just waiting for you to find it again."

- FRANK ZAPPA

Date: _____

❤️ (MY) WELL-BEING CHECK IN:
How I'm feeling

....
....
....

🙌 (MY) GRATITUDE TODAY:
What, who and things I'm grateful for

....
....
....

📅 (MY) INTENTION FOR TODAY:
What I hope/intend to accomplish or even create today?

....
....
....

🎯 (MY) GOAL FOR WHAT I'M WORKING ON AND CREATING:

....
....
....

💪 I AM:
My affirmation for today

ADDITIONAL NOTES, THOUGHTS, REFLECTIONS, VIBES AND GRATITUDE:

What are you doing to get closer to your goals, intentions, and wellness? What are the challenges you are facing? What else comes up during your day to reflect on?

www.ingramcontent.com/pod-product-compliance
Lightning Source LLC
Chambersburg PA
CBHW040409010526
44108CB00046B/2770